1

The Real Story of Count Dracula

Count Dracula is a childhood story most of us were raised on as kids. There are certain stories we liked as kids and there are certain stories we like as adults. The stories we like as kids, they change as we become adults. Our age can determine the kind of stories we like. There are many stories that are created according to our age. There are many stories we like depending on our age. The stories we are interested in have a lot to do with the age we are. Our minds comprehend to the stories that are connected to the thinking process of our brains. The thoughts of the mind come from the brain. The brain functions through the connection the brain has with the environment. The brain is the body organ that is completely responsible for the thoughts our mind thinks. The brain is the body organ that creates the mind whenever the brain thinks. The brain thinks according to how it responds to the environment a person is in at that particular time.

The environment plays a role in how the brain thinks. The brain plays a major role in how the mind is developed every time the brain thinks. Most of the time, our age determines how our brain thinks and the environment helps to shape the thoughts the brain develops. There is a difference between thinking and thoughts. Thinking is when the thoughts are in motion; thoughts are when thinking comes to a conclusion about whatever it is the brain is thinking about. This process happens faster than the speed of light. It's just like if you are driving and you are looking for something and at the moment you can't find what you are looking for than all of a sudden you come in contact with the place you are looking for, so now you stop the car. In the same way, that is how the brain works concerning the thinking that takes place in the brain. The way the brain thinks is similar to the way we act and respond when we are in a car driving down a street looking for something.

As we are driving down the street in our car looking for something, the car is in motion (the thinking of the brain), but when we find what we are looking for than we stop the car (thinking comes to a conclusion).

The factor that controls the entire process of driving the car and looking for what you are trying to find is the environment you are in as you are driving your car. In the same way, the factor that controls the entire thinking process of the brain is the environment we are in at that particular time. When our minds are driving, it is looking for a conclusion just like we are looking for the place we are trying to find: Once the brain comes to a conclusion, the car of the brain stops, which is the mind.

When we are in our cars looking for something there are two environments involved; the motion of the car and the environment that is influencing us to drive the car and to look for whatever it is we are looking for. When the brain thinks, there are two mental environments that are involved; the thinking of the brain and the environment that is influencing the brain to think. When we are looking for something when we are in our car driving down a street and we come to a stop when we find what we are looking for, we are completely responsible for the stopping of the car. When the brain is thinking, the brain is completely responsible for the conclusion the thinking of the brain has arrived to.

As the brain thinks, the brain is communicating with the environment that is controlling its thinking. Once the brain determines the best response to the environment then the brain comes to a conclusion. When the brain comes to a conclusion, than thoughts are developed; now thoughts exist. The thoughts that are developed at the conclusion of the brain are thoughts that are completely connected to the environment the brain is communicating with through the thinking process of the brain. The thinking of the brain develops and creates thoughts when the brain reaches a conclusion. The conclusion of the brain is when the thinking of the brain stops just as when we stop as we are looking for something when our car is in motion. In the same way, all of this happens in the brain, it just happens in a mental capacity rather than in a physical capacity.

This mental process is a process that is invisible because the mind is invisible; that's why science has had a very difficult time trying to understand the ability and construction of the mind. The brain has always been very easy to understand because the brain is visible. The brain has been easier to understand since the development of technology and when technology was designed to be connected to neuroscience, which is the science used to study the brain. Although, the mind is created by the thinking of the brain, once the mind is created there is a relationship that exists between the brain and the mind. This relationship is strange and complicated. The relationship between the brain and the mind doesn't happen when the brain is thinking it happens when the brain comes to a conclusion. When the brain comes to a conclusion, the relationship starts between the brain and the mind on behalf of the mind. So the mind is the first to start the relationship. Because the mind is the first to start the relationship between the brain and the mind, the mind starts the relationship through influence, which is when any person or anything causes something to happen by using the other party.

Once the brain comes to a conclusion, the thoughts the brain develops and creates, those thoughts the mind uses to influence the brain to respond to whatever the brain was trying to come to a conclusion about. The influence starts when thoughts are developed through the thinking of the brain. The mind becomes fully and completely grown when thoughts are developed and the reason why the mind becomes fully and completely grown is because when thoughts are developed, than the mind is able to influence the brain to respond. When the brain thinks, the brain doesn't influence the thinking because thinking is something that is automatic. When something happens that is automatic there is no influence involved because there is no involuntary communication. When influence is involved, than that is when voluntary communication happens and that is when someone or something can be influence to do something by the other party. When something happens automatically, there is no influence, but when something happens that isn't automatic than there is a place for influence. When the brain thinks that is something that happens automatically, but when the brain develops thoughts than that is when the influence begins.

When thoughts are developed the mind has an independence (fully and completely grown). When thoughts are developed, the mind has the ability to influence the brain. When the mind becomes completely grown, the mind has a relationship with the brain, but until than there is no relationship between the brain and the mind because there is no influence. After thoughts are developed, the mind influences the brain to respond to whatever the brain was trying to come to a conclusion about. At this stage of mental communication, the mind is in complete control of what the brain decides to do. At this stage, the decision the brain makes has everything to do with what the mind is telling it to do. Once the brain is influence by the mind than the brain influences the body to respond to the environment.

The same pattern of mental functioning takes place in the brains of adults and kids. There is no different in functioning, but there is a difference in the communication that happens between the brain and the environment before thoughts are developed. The way the brains of adults communicate with the environment is completely different from the way that the brains of kids communicate with the environment. The environment plays a role in the way the brain thinks for adults and kids as well, but the communication is different between the two and that has everything to do with the form of concept, which is the way a person is able to think. Kids think different than adults. The thinking of kids is different than the thinking of adults because the developments of their brains are different.

8

Because the development of a kid's brain is different from adults, the environment can influence the way a kid thinks about the environment concerning the things a kid is experiencing in an environment. So the environment can determine the response of the kid's actions: adults on the other hand, can determine the response they will have towards the environment concerning their actions.

The part of the brain that thinks, which is the cerebrum, is less developed as a kid than as an adult. How much the cerebrum is developed will determine how a person will think towards whatever it is in their environment they encounter. The brain continues to grow physically after birth. The size of the brain changes as we grow. So the brain is a different size as a kid than as an adult, but it is different for the software of the brain. The software of the brain is the different components in the brain that make it possible for the brain to function. Those components don't change like the hardware of the brain, which is the physical and solid structure of the brain and that is the entire outside of the brain.

The software of the brain doesn't change like the hardware of the brain does, it advances. Advancement isn't a change, advancement causes a change. The growing of the hardware of the brain has nothing at all to do with the advancement of the cerebrum, which is where the brain thinks. So thinking doesn't change, it just advances and like I said, advancement causes a change. As the hardware of the brain grows, the things that we are able to do with our body changes: as the software of the brain advances the way we respond to our environment changes, but the software stays the same, it doesn't change like the hardware of the brain. Take technology for an example, when the computer first came out it looked different than it does today, so there was a change, but the change was caused by the advancement of computer technology. It was the advancement of computer technology that changed computer technology; computer technology didn't change itself. The way computer technology is today is basically the way it was when computers started, it just advanced by the things that were add to computer technology.

The advancement of the software of the brain just adds to the way the brain thinks, but the software of the brain doesn't change because the pattern of the brain doesn't change, it just advances. Computer technology hasn't changed it just advanced.

The function (pattern) of the brain doesn't change it just advances as it learns through the environment. As the brain learns through the environment things are added to the function of the brain, but the brain continues to function the same way as it thinks, it just learns how to respond differently in different parts of a person's life. As a person lives each day the brain learns through the brains thinking. The age of the person doesn't have anything to do with the learning process of the brain it is through the thinking process that the brain learns.

The thinking process of the brain has everything to do with the learning process of the brain. The thinking process of the brain had everything to do with the environment the brain is connected to through its thinking. The environment advances the thinking of the brain and the thinking of the brain advances the thoughts of the mind. When the brain thinks, the thinking belongs to the brain, but when thoughts are developed than the thoughts belong to the mind. That goes back to what I was saying about the mind earlier concerning the mind becoming fully grown. It is just like when we are kids everything we have belongs to our parents, but the things we accumulate as we become adults they belong to us. When the brain thinks, the mind belongs to the brain, but when thoughts are developed than the brain belongs to the mind because than the mind influences the brain.

This is the pattern of the thinking of the brain with the environment added to the pattern. The environment influences the brain because the environment causes the brain to think the way it does as the brain learns from the environment, than the brain causes thinking to accrue as it is trying to determine a conclusion; once the conclusion is determined than the brain develops thoughts about the conclusion and those thoughts transforms the mind from childhood to adulthood, from immaturity to fully grown.

Not our age, but what we encounter as we live, will determine how we will respond towards something in our environment mentally, physically or both. We can respond to something in our environment mentally without responding to it physically. We respond to something in our environment mentally when our brains come to a conclusion about something. The thinking is not the response, the thinking is the determination the brain will do towards something in our environment; once thoughts are developed about the determination those thoughts are the response because those thoughts are sure about what it is that we have encountered in our environment, if our thinking isn't sure it tries to reach a conclusion so it can be sure.

Our brains learn differently as kid than as adults because we are placed in different situations as kids than as adults. The different learning has nothing to do with age in the situation. If kids experience the same situations as adults do than kids will be able to respond the same way as adults if there motor movement is as flexible as adults. Kids aren't allowed to be in some of the same situations as adults because of the decision of the parents. This is an example, in ancient times there were many kids in kingdom who were kings and there were many teenagers in ancient times who were kings and the reason why that happened is because the adult parents would allow for the kid to experience the same situation they did, so their brains were able to develop the same kind of thoughts as adults.

So that proves that the environment a person encounters will determine how much their thinking process will advance and how fast it will advance. The things a person encounter in their environment will determine how they will respond to their environment and when environments are different from each other that is also a factor in how much a person's thinking process will advance and how fast it will advance. That's the reason why people are different in the way they do things concerning what part of the world they were born and raised in. People encounter different things from one Country to another Country. In India for an example, people learn at a very young age how to handle snakes. On Facebook, I saw two kids, not teenagers, two kids catch a very large snake; now two kids in America couldn't even began to catch a snake that big, not even a small garden snake and not to mention an adult who is born here in the United States.

In India, kids can handle a cobra snake with no problem at all. Here in America they will be bitten to death. The pattern of thinking (function) between the two kids: The kids in India and the kids in the United States are the same, which is to determine a conclusion to the situation; what's different is the conclusion. Both kids will think the same way towards the cobra snake situation, but both kids will develop thoughts that will be different. The thoughts will determine how they will handle the situation concerning the cobra snake, not the thinking process.

The thinking process will make them the same in mental functioning it is the thoughts that will make them different in their mental decision.

Two Indian kids who grow up in the same environment can also have a difference in mental decision. That has everything to do with what kind of encounters their adult parents will allow for them to experience in their environment and that is the same way it is all over the world concerning the development of mental decisions. The development of mental decisions has to do with what and how much is added to the thinking process of the brain, which will determine how advance the thinking of the brain will be. The advancement of the thinking of the brain will determine how well and better one person will respond to a situation than another person and that has to do with how much we have experienced with the environment.

When we are kids, our adult parents are the people who determine what and when we will encounter what we encounter in our environment. As kids, television is something that all adult parents will allow for their kids to encounter in their environment. One thing in an environment can determine how a person will respond to something else in a different environment.

Or one thing in the same environment will determine how a person would respond to something else in the same environment.

One thing can determine how a person would respond to another thing in their environment. There are things in the environment that will cause a person's thinking process to advance differently. A person's thinking process can advance differently at different times and that has to do with how complicated a situation is a person experience. Some situations can cause a person's thinking process to advance slower in some situations and faster in other situations. What's in a person's environment that will cause their thinking process to advance fast will help them to figure out something that will cause their thinking process to advance slower.

How advance a person's thinking process is can be determined by how advance their environment is and how advanced the learning is their environment provides. An example of that is the learning culture of China. China's learning environment is much faster than any other Country. There driving system is much faster than any other Country. If we as Americans would drive a car in China we wouldn't make it to where we were going because the car we would be driving would be so destroyed from car accidents we would have, we won't be able to drive the car after a certain distance of us driving on the streets in China. The way they drive makes their thinking process concerning driving a lot more advance than our thinking process concerning driving. So we would have an accident, but they wouldn't.

So when they come to the United States and drive on our streets they are much more advanced than we are on our own streets. Their driving environment causes their thinking process to advance faster concerning driving than our driving environment, which brings me back to something that I just said in the first paragraph, which is, what's in a person's environment that will cause their thinking process to advance fast, it will help them to figure out something that will cause their thinking process to advance slower. The driving system in China will help the Chinese people who came here to America drive much better than us because their driving system is faster and ours is slower.

American kids aren't as advanced as some of the other kids in other Countries concerning the thinking process of the brain, so it is very hard to determine what is true from what isn't true concerning the things that kids watch on television. This thinking capacity shapes the way a person see's a television program as an adult and some of the same television program that adult had seen many times on television when they were kids. There were many different television programs on television when we were kids and many of those television programs are still on television today. The television program that continues to capture the attention and the excitement of kids and adults today is called Count Dracula.

As kids, we saw the Count Dracula movies as fiction. When we were kids, we saw those movies as fiction because as kids we came in contact with many things in our environment that caused our thinking process to advance much faster than the Count Dracula movies. So what we came in contact with in our environment that caused our thinking process to think much faster, it helped us as kids to determine that the Count Dracula movies we watched on television were fiction because the Count Dracula movies caused our thinking process to think much slower, than other things that we came in contact with as kids that caused our thinking process to think much faster.

What we came in contact with in our environment that was faster, it helped us as kids to understand what was much slower. An example of that, learning in school, much faster, helped us to understand something that was much slower a kids, a television program.

Although, the Count Dracula movies were fiction, it had a non-fiction side to it that we couldn't see as kids and many of us still can't see the non-fiction side to the story as adults and there is a reason for that. The environment we are in as kids will shape the way we think towards things as adults and genetics can play a factor in it as well. When a kid is introduced to something that will advance their thinking process, it will help them to understand things that will cause their thinking process to think normal. Anything that isn't advanced is normal. If a kid come in contact with something inside their environment that will cause their thinking process to advance in understanding than anything under that, they are able to understand very easily; than they will be able to piece together what is fiction about a television program that can tell them about what is non-fiction about the same television program.

When I was a kid I got involved with a group of people who studied very high science and history and I used what I learned from them to figure out other things that were on a much lower level of understanding than the science and history I learned from them. The high level of science and history I learned from this group of people, it advanced my level of learning something. When I left the group I got involved with church and I learned about another person who gave me a much higher understanding of things and that person is Jesus. Jesus took my level of understanding to a height that is higher than a mountain. So now I can understand and see many things about certain things that other people aren't able to see and television programs are one of those things.

The science and history I learned from this group influenced my mind to think in ways my mind didn't think before (advance). See I am only going back to what I was talking about concerning the mind and that is the advancement of the mind.

The science and history I learned from this group advanced my think process so much that my mind continued to think all the time and that is the reason why I think all the time now, which takes me back to something that I said earlier and that was, the environment we are in as kids will shape the way we think towards things as adults. The science and history I learned from this group as a kid, it shaped the way I think now. There are many things in our world that are design to influence us to think a certain way, regardless, if it is intellectual thinking or stupid thinking. When a person come in contact with something in their environment that is highly intellectual and they are over the top interested in it like I was in the science and history I learned from that group of people when I was a kid, than it will not only advance the thinking process of that person, but it will causes that person to think much more than they did previously.

That is how I am able to figure out what is fiction in a movie by using what is non-fiction in the movie, if what is fiction has a real meaning to it through the fiction. Sometimes a fictional movie has a non-fictional side to it. This is an example, in the New Edition Story there is a part in the story, where Bobby was on stage and it was time for Mike, Ronnie and rick to perform and Bobby didn't want to get off the stage, which the three of them forced Bobby off the stage. In the movie, Bobby grabbed a fire extinguisher hose and tried to spray it on Mike,

Ronnie and rick. In reality, Bobby didn't grab a fire extinguisher hose he grabbed a fire extinguisher. The fiction was the fire extinguisher hose the non-fiction was the fire extinguisher. If you look closely at the picture, the fire extinguishing hose Bobby had wasn't long enough to reach the stage. Through that, a person who was watching that television program could see that the fire extinguisher hose was the fiction, but because of Bobby's known past behavior, he would have done something like that, but with a more reasonable device, a device that fits the situation.

The movie Count Dracula, because of his character in the movie, he would do the things the movie says he did, but in a reasonable fashion, which is a fashion that makes sense to the minds of people. If you remember the story, Count Dracula bit people on the neck for the purpose of feeding. When a person bits someone that means that two people are coming together to do something for a cause. In the scientific world, back during the time of Count Dracula, two people came together for purpose of doing something that was completely connected to the world of science.

Science was something that Count Dracula was interested in a great deal, so he had a very high interest in the world of science. The scientific world is what advanced his thinking process more as an adult, but the scientific world also advanced his thinking process as a kid. Count Dracula was a nobleman, which means his family was also noble and they were noble because they were also involved with the scientific world and they introduced Count Dracula to the scientific world when he was a kid. This take you back to the end of page 5 and page 6.

During the time of Count Dracula there were many people who were involved in the scientific world and the reason why it was called the the scientific world, which is what it is called today, is because there were many different kinds of science being studied and practiced in England during that time. The people who practiced science in England during the time of Count Dracula were considered as nobleman and they are also considered as nobleman in our Country today, but under a different identity. Nobleman in England, during that time and even now are considered as the upper class society because of the life style they were able to live because of their accomplishments.

The English scientists were extremely intelligent men. Many people from all around the world went to England to learn science because the English people learned to master the practice along with the study of the sciences that was a plateau of English society. The English learned their part in the sciences through the Germans. The Germans were also very intelligent people in the sciences. To tell you the truth, I don't know which society was smarter in the study and practice of the sciences.

The practice of the sciences existed long before the Germans and the English became involved in the sciences. Nothing starts on its own. Something always existed because of something else. People have always gotten their ideals to do something from someone else. The difference between the two is one group may have advanced better and more than the other group, but their purpose is always the same and that is to better humanity civilization for all the people who are under their intellect, in other words, for people who aren't as smart. There have always been people who have looked after the welfare of others who are less fortunate and the people who have studied and practiced the sciences were those people who looked after the less fortunate, even, if the less fortunate were people in their own family.

The less fortunate isn't always the people who are poorer or less smart; they are also people who aren't capable of doing something that talented people can. Those were the first people who were helped by the first people who studies and practiced the sciences. They were actually forced to study and practice the sciences to save one of their loves ones from any disease they may have had that put their lives in jeopardy. They were influenced to study and practice the sciences because of their intellect they discovered by doing different kinds of other practices in which they had success in doing. So they put that intellectual energy towards something that would save the lives of their love ones who were the people who were less fortunate. The first people to study and practice the sciences were the ancient Africans.

The Africans use to do a lot of experiments in the ancient world. The Africans were the first group of people who started experiments with the sperm and egg of many species. Some of the experiments the Africans did in ancient times were known by scientists in modern times. The people who were very familiar with the experiments of the ancient Africans were the English scientists in London England.

The ancient Africans were the first people to experience the study and practices of the sciences; back than there was just a different name for the same sciences that are practiced today. In the scientific world, there is always a particular scientific study that scientists give more attention to than other scientific studies. In the ancient world of science, the scientific study that scientists would focus more on was what we call today as chimera genetics. This particular science had captured the attention of many famous scientists in the past. This was a science the ancient Africans were highly interested in through their extreme curiosity of the existence of mankind.

For centuries, the curiosity of mankind has interested many people outside of the science world because people are a species that other people deal with the most. Anything people deal with the most that is what they are probably interested in the most. People have always been interested in each other, regardless, if they are involved in science or not. Something that people are interested in the most will influence people to focus on it the most than other things that also have a focus of interest. People have always had the most interest in something that resembles them the most and most of the time that is something or someone they have a connection with the most. People have a connection with other people the most out of all the other things they have a connection with. The connection that people have with each other is what influenced many scientists in the past to focus on the science of chimera genetics and it is also the reason why this kind of science was created by man.

This is a kind of science that influenced many scientists to create many different species other than the species they were already familiar with. Through chimera genetics, people were able to create different species from the species that already exist. Some of those created species will carry the resemblance of the other species that were used to make the created species and that was something that many scientists experience and that is something that anyone would experience who is involved with that kind of science. The ancient Africans involvement with the science of chimera genetics influence many other scientists who came after them to be interested in that particular science along with the other existing sciences. In some case, the things that an earlier group of people were interested in would influence a later group of people to be interested in the same things. Sometime people do that because they are interested in the same thing or because they will try and take it to a different level than those who did it before them.

In some ages, people who were different from other people because of their talent, they would record everything including the things they were able to accomplish through their work. The ancient Egyptians were people who would record everything that happened in the world. They were the people who brought the scientific world to another level and the level they brought science to be is seen in many of the practices that are done in the science world today.

Many people who came after them, who were interested in the same things, they advanced in a great way what the Egyptians started. The Egyptians weren't the only and first people to get involved with the scientific world. But they too brought what they learned from the science of past scientists to a much higher level than those who were before them. In the same way, there were many scientists who came after the Egyptians who advanced the sciences on a much higher level than the Egyptians and those people were the Germans and the English.

The Germans and the English have always respected the ancient Egyptians at their many accomplishments, especially, the accomplishments they made in the scientific world. Matter of fact, the work the ancient Egyptians did in the scientific world wasn't only discussed among the Germans and the English, but the ancient Egyptians were also discussed among many other scientists who were outside of their culture.

The reason why I say their culture is because two thousand years ago, the Germans and the English had the same culture because they were actually the same people, but in different parts of the world. Many people from Germany migrated to England and when they arrived in England they ended up taking the land from the English people and the Germans who migrated there were much more powerful than the English people who were already living in England at the time.

The group of Germans who invaded England were called the Anglo-Saxons. The Anglo-Saxons were some very intelligent people. At the time they invaded England, science was a main source of study in Germany. At that time, there were many people in Germany who were interested in science.

At the time the Germans invaded England, there was only one class of people in Germany and they were highly intelligent people. Because there was only one class of people in Germany at the time, everyone in Germany was on the same level and they were interested in the same things and that interest was science. Although, there was one group or class of people in Germany at the time the Anglo-Saxons invaded England, there were a few different tribes or groups of people. Just like it has always been among people, Germany had a system of hierarchy, which means in definition, higher and lower positions of power.

The Anglo-Saxons were the lowest rank in the hierarchy, but they were the smartest people in the rank. They were a group of people who were feared the most by the people who were of the highest rank in Germany at the time and they were known as the Uradels. The Uradels were a selfish tribe of people who didn't want to share their power and privileges with anyone else who lived in the German kingdom and the Anglo-Saxons were the tribe who should have had a share of what the Uradels had because the Anglo-Saxons contributed a lot to Germany through the world of science. The Anglo-Saxons were run off by the Uradels, when the Anglo-Saxons began to feel unwelcome by the Uradels.

Once the Anglo-Saxons left Germany they traveled west to the land of England. Once they learned the military defense and offence of the English army than they decided to invade it and take it over.

When the Anglo-Saxons conquered the English than the Anglo-Saxons made the English people a part of their culture by interbreeding with them. That's how one nation was able to take over another nation without experiencing rebellion from the nation that was conquered. It's just like if one nation would have kids with another nation they conquered, the conquered nation will eventually accept the nation they were conquered by because now there is a positive connection between the two nations, which are the kids they had produced between each other.

Kids can play a major part in the relationship of two people. In some cases or I will say in many cases, the kids are the reason why two parents will refuse to become enemies and are forced to be friends. That was how it was between the Anglo-Saxons and the English people they had conquered in England. For centuries, that was the method that nations would use towards other nations they had conquered, so there won't be any rebellion from the nation that was conquered. That was how the Anglo-Saxons won the acceptance of the English people they had conquered in England.

After the Anglo-Saxons conquered the English people who were living in England at the time, than the Anglo-Saxons begin to share their scientific learning experience with the English people; a system of learning the English people were familiar with, but didn't have any interest in because of their inability to master such a learning skill. If there is something that a person can't master because they have a difficult time learning what they can't master, than that is something they won't have any interest in and the English people didn't have any interest in any forms of science because it was a very difficult learning skill for them to learn.

For centuries, people were able to master the basic things of survival, which is also a form of science because learning is involved. Anything a person learns is a form of science because the only thing science is is learning about the environment a person is a part of at a particular time in their lives.

Thinking is a science, but it is the lowest form of science that will introduce a person to the highest form of science through the advancement the thinking process of the brain is able to elevate to as the thinking process learns to adapt to the form of science, the brain is communicating with at a particular time, which take you back to the earlier part of this story. The basic forms of science, which is something a person learns for the purpose of survival, is and was the form of science that all people are able to master, unless they have some kind of mental problem that would stop them from learning. The basic form of science was the form of science the people in England learned and mastered, but any other form of science outside of that they didn't have any success in learning until they merged with the Anglo-Saxons.

Eventually, the English people had adapted the Anglo-Saxons culture, which included the things the Anglo-Saxons were interested in. The culture of a person involves everything a person does in their live on a day to day basis and everything that is connected to what a person does on a day to day basis. The things that are connected to what a person does are the things that happen as a result of what a person does. There are always results from something that is done. What is done is the person's culture and the result is what is connected to something that is done.

What the Anglo-Saxons had a habit of doing constantly was to isolate their presence from the presence of other for the purpose of scientific experiments. Their scientific experiments was their culture because scientific experiments was something the Anglo-Saxons did a lot of and the things that happened as a result was what was connected to their culture.

Scientific experiments were something the Anglo-Saxons became involved in on a regular basis. So scientific experiments were something the Anglo-Saxons did all the time. Just like scientists do today, which is to separate their presence from the presence of other people for the purpose of scientific experiments; the Anglo-Saxons did the same thing. Matter of fact, it was the Anglo-Saxons who started that kind of scientific environment and it was created by them, so the people who were doing the experiment could do their experiment without any distractions. That was the reason why that kind of experimental environment was first started, but the English people used that kind of experimental environment for a different reason from the reason why the Anglo-Saxons used that kind of experimental environment in which they actually started.

The English scientists used the experimental environment also for the same reason the Anglo-Saxons used it for, but they added another reason for using it and that was to keep the scientific learning from the intellect of other people and also to keep their experiments away from the knowledge of others, so others couldn't get involved with what they did unless they were invited.

The same reason the English scientists used the Anglo-Saxons experimental environment is the same exact reason scientists use that kind of method today in scientific research. Sometimes one group of people may be much better than another group of people in the same area of study and most of the time, the people who are better are the people who were taught by the people who they became better than. The reason why that happens is because the group that became better is the group that had a different kind of thinking towards something that both groups of people had an interest in.

The Anglo-Saxons and the English had the same interest when the two groups begin to have the same culture and that interest was science. The Anglo-Saxons were the people who taught the English how to study the sciences.

Each science had a different way of study and that is the reason why all sciences don't have the same kind of study, but the study of one science can help the study of another science. One science can help a scientist in another field of scientific study because some sciences support other sciences. A scientist could probably learn more about one science from the study of another science and sometimes a scientist can use one science to advance his thinking in another science. That was something the English scientists were able to do that the German scientists couldn't do and for that reason, the English scientists accomplished much more than the German scientists in the scientific world.

Although, it was through the Anglo-Saxons that the English people were able to learn science, it was the English people who became much better in science than the Anglo-Saxons and all of the other people in the past who practice the sciences. Every scientist has their favorite form of science and their favorite form of science was also the favorite form of science for the scientists who practice science before they did. Most of the time what a person is interested in and what they show the most interest in is what someone else before them had an interest in and what become the later person's favorite interest is something a previous person had a favorite interest in.

What the Anglo-Saxons scientists had a favorite interest in is what the English scientists had a favorite interest in. Back then, the system of the study of the sciences was different compared to the way the system of the study of the sciences are today. Back than; a scientist was involved in every form of science or involved in more than one science that depended on the scientist. So back than; a scientist could be involved with how many sciences he wanted to be involved in just as long as his intellect could handle the different studies.

If his mind could handle the different studies and he was interested in the different studies, than he was allowed to study the different sciences he had an interest in.

Most of the English scientists who came into the scientific world after the Anglo-Saxons, they were interested in the science of chimera genetics. Matter of fact, chimera genetics was the favorite practice of science to the English Scientists. It was their favorite form of science because it was the favorite form of science for many other scientists who practice science before them.

The extreme interest in the science of chimera genetics goes back to the beginning of science and back during the beginning of science, the science of chimera genetics was used only on humans because humans were the complete focus of people in ancient times. At one time and for a long time, the science of chimera genetics was practiced through interracial breeding, but it was always monitored by the person who was responsible for the practice and that form of practice is what was used to create the many different races of people there are today.

Matter of fact, the first form of human chimera genetics practice was done for the purpose of trying to start a new race of people. That was a form of practice that started in ancient times and adapted by many scientists in future times. That form a scientific research became a big interest to the Germans during the time of Hitler and that influenced Hitler to get his scientists involve in trying to create a new race of people who would have blond hair and blue eyes. Hitler thought that was how the master race should look because that was how most of the Anglo-Saxons looked who conquered England in the 5th century and the Anglo-Saxons were a group of people who have always been admired by the German people because

38

in their time they were the smartest Germans in Germany in the 5th century.

The main reason the Anglo-Saxons were admired by the German people was because they were the people who caused science to be what it is today and their favorite science of interest was also the science of chimera genetics. Intellectual people, who were the people who have always been used in the scientific world and who were the people who started the scientific world, were constantly interested in changing the human race from what they have always known the human race to be.

Some scientists have gone to the extent of trying to merge together the cells of two completely different species and the ancient Egyptians were the first people to do that kind of experiment and that's the reason why there are picture carvings of two different beings that share the same body in there form of recording used in hieroglyphics.

Hieroglyphics was a form of writing the ancient Egyptians used to communicate and most of all, to record something that they had knowledge of that had happened.

They mainly used Hieroglyphics to record things so history knowledge could be pasted down to future generations just like the people in the history world write down past history so that people in future times could learn about the things that happened in the past.

That form of recording started from the ancient Egyptians and adapted by all other people in future times. Through their Hieroglyphics, which many people in past time would go down to Egypt to learn and study; the scientists who came after the ancient Egyptians learned what science the ancient Egyptian had more of and interest for and when many kingdoms learned to interpret the Hieroglyphics of the ancient Egyptians they learned that their favorite scientific study was chimera genetics. So through the ancient Egyptians, the science of chimera genetics became the favorite science for many other scientists who studies science after the ancient Egyptians.

The people who had the most interest in the ancient Egyptians were the Anglo-Saxons. When the English people became a part of the German culture through the Anglo-Saxons, the English began to develop a relationship with the German people, but it wasn't the entire people of England who began to form a relationship with the Germans, it was just the English people who became a part of the scientific world through their Anglo-Saxon ancestors. When the Germans and the English began to study together than what part of the world the Germans were interested in, the English people became interested in as well. For that reason, it was the interest the Germans had in ancient Egypt that influenced the English people to have an interest in ancient Egypt. That caused a lot of conflict between the Germans and the English, which was what the movie "Raiders of the Lost Ark" was based on.

The conflict the Germans had with the English over the study of Egypt is how that movie was made, so the Raiders of the Lost Ark is one of those stories that have a non-fiction part to the story because it was based on the conflict between Germany and England over Egypt.

The Anglo-Saxons scientists and the English scientists learned a lot from the Egyptian Hieroglyphics and the things they learned from the ancient Egyptians through their Hieroglyphics taught them a lot about the study of science, which the Anglo-Saxons scientists and the English scientists copied and advance by bring what they learned to a much higher level.

The English scientists were the scientists who created the names that are used for the different sciences today. The scientific world that scientists in America are a part of is only a carbon copy of the scientific world the English scientists were a part of, so everything is done the same way.

Like I said, the English scientists, just like the Anglo-Saxons scientists had their favorite form of scientific study and that was chimera genetics. That kind of science was the favorite science of Count Dracula. People who were involved and who had a major role in scientific research in England during the time of Count Dracula were people who had an important statues or position in England during that time.

Today, anyone can become a part of the scientific world by studying science in college, which is how a person starts off in the scientific world and how a person started in the scientific world back during the time of Count Dracula. Today, anyone can become a part of the scientific world when they go to college and major in a specific program of science. A person who comes from a very low income community can become a part of the scientific world today, but back during the time of Count Dracula, the only person who could be a part of the scientific world were the nobleman of England. They were the only people during that time that could learn and practice science. Science was something that was preserved and treasured.

The English scientists were interested in everything that had to do with the world. They were very inquisitive people. They also were people who recorded everything just like the ancient Egyptians did. Chimera genetics is a science that is very interesting out of all the other sciences that exist because if a person is able to master it than they can find out the deep thing about the creation of humans, animals and insects. The English Scientists tried to find out everything there was to know about the creation of two cells and that was the focus of Count Dracula for years into his studies.

The merging of two cells is what creates conception in every form of life in every species. It is the merging of two cells that produces any form of life. In order for two cells to merge, one cell has to be the aggressor. The cell that is the aggressor is the cell that initiates the merging. In the human race, it is the male sperm that is the aggressor and through its aggressions is why it searches for the egg that is inside the woman's womb.

The male sperm is the cell that is always active and it is active because of the movement it does inside the woman's womb when it enters the woman's womb through sexual intercourse. In every species, the cell of one species is more aggressive than the cell in another species and what happens as a result, one cell searches for the other cell, just like what happens between the sperm cell of a man and the egg cell of the woman.

When it has to do with conception, which happens in every species, one cell acts different than the other cell concerning aggression. The function of conception is something that has amazed scientists in every field of science. Aggression between any two living cells happens for a reason. The cell that is aggressive toward another cell is aggressive toward the other cell because there is some kind of attraction that influences the one cell to be aggressive towards the other cell. This was a theory that was known to scientists years ago in the past and scientists today were able to actually see the merging together of two living cells through medical technology.

Through medical technology, a person is actually able to see the complete function of conception from beginning to end and that was something the earlier scientists didn't have the ability to see because of the lack of technology.

Although, the earlier scientists didn't have the technology to see with their own eyes the start and the end of conception, they know that it happened the same way that scientists are able to see today with their own eyes. How did the earlier scientists know the function of conception from beginning to end without technology? The earlier scientists would create the same kind of biological environment outside of the body that existed inside the womb of a woman and then they took a sperm cell of a man and the egg cell of a woman and they put them at a certain distance away from each other and they reacted the same way because the environment was the same as the environment of a woman's womb. So what the male sperm cell does in the woman's womb is what that male sperm cell did in the environment that was created to be identical to the woman's womb. If an environment is the same as the environment the cell is used to than the cell will act the same way.

Through an artificial biological environment made to be exactly the way a woman's womb is is how the earlier scientists were able to see and know how the function of conception happens from beginning to end and some scientists still use that form of experiment to determine how things happen between two things they are studying. The start of conception between two cells is the same in human and animals, but it is a little different concerning insects. So insects were created a little differently than humans and animals.

This is some science on the creation of insects. Insects were created in a different way compared to the way that Adam and animals were created. Adam and animals were created the same way, but for different purposes. Adam and animals were created from the dirt of the earth. Adam was created from the chemical process of the soil, which was when the soils atoms were changed a number of times to produce many different stages of molecules, until the molecules went into its final stage and produced a substance called skin. Adam's skin was the only human skin that was considered as a substance because it was created from something that wasn't organic. Soil is a substance, but not organic because it doesn't live. Anything that doesn't live is created from a substance.

Why? Because it took a material to created it and soil is a material. God used a substance to create something that lives. So Adams skin was a substance as well as organic. But all the people who came from Adam, their skin was organic not a substance because when they were created they were created from another living organism, (human being) and not from soil. But their beginning was the soil because they came from a man and woman, (Adam and Eve), who were created from the soil. Adam was bio-chemical. Because Adam was a living organism, he was bio and because he was brought forth from a certain process he was chemical and the process was when the soil kept changing until Adam's body was formed.

Animals were also formed from the soil. The first animals were created from the soil of the earth, which was the first stage of the creation of animals. The second stage was the force interbreeding. The third stage was the experimental creation and the fourth and final stage was sexual interbreeding.

All of this happened about twelve thousand years ago. If you were taking a history course or some kind of science of nature course, you will learn that man is one, two or maybe three million years old.

Some courses will probably give you a much later date then that, but that isn't true. Man is no more than twelve thousand years old and that's all. Insects are about eleven thousand years old. Insects came from man and animals. When Adam and animals were created, there were no insects for about a thousand years. Insects were created when people and animals begin to die.

Insects came from bacteria. Bacteria, is created from something that decays. Back during this time people didn't bury people after they died. They would just let the body lay there and decay. As the body decayed, the body produced bacteria. Bacteria, is something that travels in the air that lives. This is going to be hard to explain, but I am going to try to explain it so you can understand it. Each speck or each tiny, tiny, tiny dot of bacteria contains only one cell. So say you have an invisible cloud of bacteria.

The reason why I say invisible is because bacteria, is something that you can't see with the naked eye, you can only see it with a microscope. Say you have an invisible cloud of bacteria that contains one hundred specks or dots of bacteria. In those dots of bacteria, which are cells, there are no cells in those dots of bacteria. Each dot is just one cell by itself with no other cells inside it.

Whereas, if you take the cell of a human or an animal, inside each cell there are hundreds, thousands, or even millions of cells inside one cell. Bacteria cells are one cell with no other cells inside it.

They are cells that can either fertilize or be fertilize. When bacteria first formed, it only fertilized, it couldn't be fertilized. It's just like when a man's sperm fertilizes a woman's egg.

When a body would decay back then and even now, it would create bacteria. Bacteria, because it is alive, it can attach itself to another cell that is alive. This is what happened, which caused insects to come forth. The cell of the bacteria would attach itself to the cell of a person or an animal that was living.

This would happen when the person or the animal would inhale the bacteria as they breathe, which would kill the person or the animal in a matter of days. The cells from the bacteria would attach to the cells that were inside the person or the animal. The cells from the bacteria would fertilize the cells of the person or the animal that would eventually die from the bacteria. The cells from the bacteria and the cells from the human or the animal would eventually   detach from the human or the animal and become an insect.

When the cell from the bacteria would fertilize the cell from the human or the animal, the cells, inside the cell of the human or animal wouldn't multiply, because they didn't have any other cell to mate with because the cell of the bacteria was a cell with no other cells inside it. So the cells that were in the cell of the human would be the cells that would create the insect and that's the reason why insects are small.

The more cells multiply, the bigger the organism will be. The more cells there are the bigger the organism will be. For an example, when the sperm of the man fertilizes the egg of a woman, the cells inside the cell of the man will mate with the cells inside the cell of the woman and the cells inside the cell will multiply and become thousands or even millions of cells and that's the reason why we grow to become big.

The more cells there are the bigger the organism will become. Because the cell of the bacteria has no cells inside it, the cells that were in the cell of the human were the cells that were used to create the insect and that's the reason why insect are so small.

Let me add, the cells that are in a single cell of a cell that is in the sperm of a man are called genes and they are in the center of each cell, which is called the nucleus.

But now since insects exist they multiply by mating just as we do. Now, insects aren't created the way they were first created. Why? That's something only God knows. I am not sure, but to take a guess I would think it is because we use the method of burying the dead now.

In London England, between the 13th and 18th century, there were a lot of doctors and scientists. London England was the place where our educational system started. The different courses a person has to take to receive a degree in college started in London England. Many things had been changed in the educational system since then. The reason for the change was because many classes or courses were add towards a particular degree or school subject, but the educational system started in London England. The people in London England, who were responsible for that, were very smart people. They were called the brilliant minds of history.

Many things happened in England after the Anglo-Saxons invasion. The changes that were made in England after the invasion were caused completely by the Anglo-Saxons. The reason for the change was because the Anglo-Saxons forced the English people to adapt to the traditions of their culture. That is something that happens when a group of people are conquered by another group of people. The people who do the conquering, they always force the people who were conquered to summit to their rules and regulations and that always include the traditions of the culture of the conquering nation.

That was something Mohammed did when he conquered the Middle East. He forced many people to surrender to Islam. When a nation is conquered by another nation, sometimes the people who were conquered surrender automatically to the rules and regulations of the conquering nation to avoid unpleasant treatment.

Some nations are extremely cruel to the nation they have conquered, especially, at the beginning of the conquering because in some cases, the nation that is being conquered is a nation that is just as strong or almost as strong as the nation who is in the process of conquering them.

In the conquering situation between the Anglo-Saxons and the English; the Anglo-Saxons were able to conquer the English without any fatal human casualties and that happened because of two reasons. The first reason was that the Anglo-Saxons and the English people at the time were very mild mannered people. Both groups of people were more timid than violent and that was the reason why the Anglo-Saxons left Germany quietly, rather than violently.

If the Anglo-Saxons wanted to, they could have fought back against the Uradels and won because they were admired more than the Uradels and the admiration a group of people have towards another group of people is power alone. Admiration is more than enough power to influence a group of people to take their side against another group of people who are the aggressors and that was something the Anglo-Saxons could have done to the Uradels, but instead they left at the request of the Uradels.

The second reason was that the Anglo-Saxons intelligence is what controlled their behavior. Most of the time people who are highly intelligent they are the people with the most reasoning. They are the people who are the most civilized and peaceful.

A person who is violent isn't intelligent; they may be smart, but not intelligent. When a person is smart, they are smart in the mind, not the heart. The mind is what produces violence not intelligence.

Intelligence comes from wisdom and wisdom is a spiritual substance that forms in the heart, not in the mind. When a person is smart and just smart, they aren't logical people because logic doesn't come from smartness, logic comes from intelligence. That's the reason why a smart person makes a lot of mistakes in their personal lives, whereas, an intelligence person doesn't.

Logic is something that will influence a person to do the things that are right, which will cause a person to avoid mistakes and logic is something that exist only in the heart and not in the mind. Our minds are against us and our hearts are on our side. Our mind will tell us to do the things that are wrong and our hearts will tell us to do the things that are right. It is smartness that will cause a person to do something brilliant at times or in situations the mind has adapted to. But intelligence will cause a person to do what is right all the time because intelligence comes from logic and logic is nothing but wisdom.

Logic is something that will causes a person to have reasoning. Reasoning is something a person has to have that will give them the ability to be fair with others they come in contact with on a daily basis. It's possible for a person to be logical towards someone in whom they are trying to conquer. The way the person treats the person in whom they are trying   to   conquer will determine if the person who is trying to do the conquering is logical or not. A person who is logical is very easy to get along with and they have good intentions concerning everything they do, regardless, if what they are doing seems bad.

The Anglo-Saxons had a very good intent and reason to conquer England from the English people and that was the reason why they conquered it. At the time, the Anglo-Saxons were stronger than the English because of their intelligence. When the Anglo-Saxons conquered the English they did it with their intelligence rather than with brutality. The Anglo-Saxons were able to do that to the English people because the English people were symbolic to kids when the Anglo-Saxons invaded England.

55

Because of their low intelligence, the English people actually needed help and assistance from another nation that were able to take care of themselves in a much better way than the English. The Anglo-Saxons actually made the living conditions of the English people better in every way. The Anglo-Saxons felt sorry for the English people because of their living conditions. So when they took the land away from the English it was just like taking something from a baby, than fix it and give it back, which was kind of how it was after the invasion.

When the English went under the rule of the Anglo-Saxons everything began to change for the English people in an instant.

The English people began to be much better equipped in their living conditions from the many positive things they learned from the Anglo-Saxons. The Anglo-Saxons shared every positive resource they had with the English people and it advanced the thinking process of the English people tremendously. Their advancement in their thinking process influenced them to handle their environment much better than what they were used to. Learning something different that is much higher than what a person is used to knowing will cause a change in a person's thinking process that will causes a person's thoughts to develop on a higher level than it was previously on and that is what happened to the English people after they began to learn from the Anglo-Saxons. That is something that will happen to anyone who learns something that is on a higher scale of learning than they are used to.

Once the living conditions changed for the English people concerning the way they now interacted with their environment, than the Anglo-Saxons introduced them to what they considered the passion of their lives and that was the scientific world.

When a person knows about something, but they are unable to adjust to it, than it is just like they haven't been introduce to it, but when they are able to adjust to it, than they are introduced to it. The English people were familiar with the science the Anglo-Saxons began to teach them, but they weren't able to adjust to it because of the lower level of intellect they had at the time when the Anglo-Saxons had invaded England.

When a person is familiar with something and they aren't able to adjust to it, which is when they don't know how to use what they are familiar with, than it takes a person who has adjusted, to teach the other person what they weren't able to adjust to.

Science was something the English people weren't adjusted to because they didn't have the intellect needed to learn the science and use the science they were familiar with. Both the Anglo-Saxons and the English grow together in the development of science after 500 A.D. When there are a group of people in a particular region and one group has conquered the other group and the group that was conquered is much large in number than the group that did the conquering, than eventually that group that did the conquering will eventually merge with the group they had conquered and the name of the conquering group diminishes, although, that group is still among the group they conquered.

That's what happened many years after the invasion of England by the Anglo-Saxons and that is the reason why the Anglo-Saxons aren't identified as a group of people in England today.

This is an example, in America there are the Caucasians, the Afro-Americans, the Polish, the Italians and so forth. The reason why is because as time went forward in America all four races had a large number of people, so neither group couldn't take away the identity of the other groups. So now all four races have an identity here in America.

Today, the English people have an identity in England, but the Anglo-Saxons have no identity, although, they are still there. For that reason, the science advancement that happened in England didn't only happen by the English, it also happened by the Anglo-Saxons, but the Anglo-Saxons don't get any credit because they don't have an identity in England anymore. The Anglo-Saxons were actually the group of people who are responsible for what science had done in England. Many of the scientists who contributed to what we see today in our societies were German.

The Germans were the smartest Caucasians back than and they are the smartest Caucasians today. If the Anglo-Saxons wouldn't have invaded England, than England wouldn't have the credit they have today towards our educational system.

As science advance and became more popular, many people in England began to gravitate to it. In the 13th century, the only people who were invited to learn science were the upper class society. They were the people who science belonged to in England because they were the people who first experienced with the practice of science and they were the only people who were allowed to not only learn science, but to practice with science as well.

Science eventually became a form of education, so science wasn't only identified as a form of practice it was beginning to be identified as a form of education. The reason why the sciences begin to be identified as a form of education is because there were a very large number of people who had become involved with the learning and practice of science.

During the time of Count Dracula, everyone in the upper class was involved with science to one degree or another. Science was learned and practiced only by the upper class and it was kept away from the poor class of people in England.

The learning of science was something that was passed down just like a royal position is passed down from the parents to the kids. Science was something that was passed down from the parents to the kids. When science became the main focus to the upper class people then they decided to get their kids involved in science at a very early age. This advanced the thinking process of the brains of many kids in England during that time. This learning system that the kids became a part of through their parents caused their thinking capacity to excel the thinking capacity of other kids who had a much lower learning environment.

Like I said in the earlier part of this writing, the environment plays a role in how advance a person's thinking process becomes, but the brain plays a major role, so the brain is much more important than the environment when learning is concern. The brain has to be able to adjust to whatever the brain is learning from the environment a person is in at a particular time.

A person's brain has an easier time adjusting to the environment when they are kids, rather than when they are adults.

If a person tries to learn a different language when they are an adult, it is much harder to learn the different language as an adult than as a kid because when a person is a kid their thinking isn't developed it has to be developed.

When a kids thinking is being developed their brain is adjusting to the first thing it encounters. The first thing it encounters will shape the way the kid thinking and the way the kids begins to think, that's the way their thinking will remain. Everything a kid learns at the beginning of their learning is supported by the other thinking they will learn later on as a kid.

Why? Because everything in a person's environment agrees with each other. For that reason, one thing can teach a kid how to use and adjust to another thing. In our society, when we eat, we use a plate, fork, spoon and knife. If a kid is taught to use a fork first than the experience with the fork will help them to use the spoon and the experience with the spoon will help them to use the knife because the experience between the three objects are the same.

But when the kid becomes an adult and they try to use chop sticks to eat the same kind of food they would use a fork, spoon and knife for, than they are helpless.

They are helpless because they don't know how to use chop sticks; they don't know how to use chop sticks because the objects they are used to using weren't design in experience to teach the person how to use chop sticks. The different environments aren't the same concerning the skills that each environment offers for eating. The skills that are developed for eating are different in both environments. So one thing doesn't support the other thing because one thing doesn't teach the person how to use the other thing they cannot use.

The fork, spoon and knife don't teach a person how to use chop sticks. But a person who is taught to use chop sticks they may be able to use a fork, spoon and knife with no problem at all because the thinking process of using chop sticks is much more advanced than the thinking process for using a fork, spoon and knife.

That takes me back to what I said earlier about the driving system in china compared to the driving system in America.

When a kid learns something, whatever it is they are learning it will help than to learn other things that relate (supports) what they are learning at that particular time. If they go into another environment that is different than they will have to learn all over again and that is what an adult experience when they learn something inside an environment that their brains aren't adjusted to.

63

That's why it is good to teach a kid as many different things as the parent can, so they don't have to learn something over again that they should have already learned that is in their own culture.

Whatever a kid learns that is what shapes them and whatever shapes them that is what they adjust to, anything else outside of that they have to learn over again. That's the reason why most people have to learn over again when they go to another Country that has a different environment than what they are used to. There is a theory that isn't true and you should see that already through what you just read. The theory is that it is harder for a person to learn something new when they are adults than it is when they are kids. That theory isn't true we all have to learn over again when we encounter something that our brains aren't adjusted to, regardless, if the person is an adult or a kid.

A better way to word that theory is to say, teach a kid everything you want that kid to know, so they don't have to learn all over again because it is hard for anyone to learn something over again if the brain have been programed to adjust to a particular environment.

When our brains are programed that is the reason why it is hard to learn something that doesn't fit in with the programming of our brains because there is nothing in our programming that can help us do or use something our brains aren't programmed to do or use and when there is nothing in our programming that doesn't relate (support) to what we can't do or use.

In England, during the time of Count Dracula, kids were forced to get involved with science by their parents who were already involved with science. That prepared those kids thinking process to adjust to anything that was lower in learning than the science they were taught at an early age, just like the Chinese people who come here can adjust to our driving system.

The development of the sciences in England influenced the same people who were involved in science to create a system of learning that still exist to this day and it will continue to exist as long as this world remains and this system of learning was called and it is called today as an education. The learning of the different sciences influenced the scientists to develop a pattern of learning that caused a person to engage in steps of learning.

From introduction to advancement in the same area of scientific study, which is how the school system is set up today and that was created by the English. The same system that is used today in the educational system concerning what a person has to learn in an orderly form was created and used by the English in the 13th century, the only difference was there was only one particular form of study and that was science, but many different fields of scientific study. Than as time went forward other subjects were added to the educational system of England and those subjects were, Mathematics, Law, English, Music, Dance, Geography, Metal and Wood Shop, Speech Therapy, Writing and some others.

Once many other subjects were added to the educational system of England than the educational system was used to birth the school system and the college system. Both of these systems started in England.

America only added a small portion to the educational system compared to what the English did. The way our educational system is today, it's the same way the educational system was in England between the 13th and 18th century, believe it or not.

The English people were some brilliant people when it had to do with planning, that's why I am completely surprised that America was able to defeat the British in the American Revolutionary War. I am surprised we won that war. The only thing I have to say about that is God was truly on our side against them because we shouldn't have won that war.

Once many different subjects were added to the education of the sciences, then the education of the sciences were converted into school and college. This form of education influenced the upper class to invite and let other people of other classes to become involved in the learning system that the upper class people had stopped them from learning for a long time.

After other classes of people were allowed to learn from the system of learning the upper class people had created, there was still a large ratio different in the number of upper class people getting an education from the number of other classes of people getting an education.

There was still a large bias in the educational system in England. The place in England where the advancement of the educational system started was London. Before the the educational system started in London, science was something that was studied by people all over England. England is the Country, just like America is a Country that has many states and cities. England is the Country and London is the city. At one time science was practiced all over England by the upper class people of England, but once science advanced through the brilliant minds who practiced science than all the scientists decide to come together to share their ideals to bring science to another level and the place they decided to come together was London.

Once the scientists throughout the Country came together that influence them to get other intellectual people involved in the circle and that drew the attention of other people who had a talent and skill in a completely different area of learning and study that had nothing at all to do with science. They were also subjects of study that other scientists were interested in and wanted to learn.

When these intelligent and brilliant minds came together than that was when other subjects were added to the world of science, although, they didn't have anything to do with science. As they began to put their ideals together their ideals influenced them to create a system from the learning system they already had.

Like I said earlier, the upper class people were the people who started to study science first and in the beginning, it was only a few of them who participated in the practice and study of science and they were the rulers and those who had brilliant minds who were assistance to the rules and the rulers were the King, Queen, Prince, Princess, Duke, Duchess, Marquis, Earl and Counts. These were the early rules and the first rules that were over the normal and regular people in England. These were the people and the only people who studies and practice science in England between the 13th and the 18th century; no one else was allowed to learn science.

There were people who held these positions all over England, so there were different kingdoms all over England and the people I just mentioned were the people who ruled and ran the kingdoms.

The king was always the overseer of all the people who ruled with him. The king also had an interested in science, but he wasn't the person who would conduct the practices. The people who would conduct the practices were Marquis, Earls and Counts. The person's name was placed in front of the name of the title the person held, like Count Dracula for instance. Count was the title and Dracula was the name of the person who held the title.

This structure didn't take place until the 16th century. This time in English history was when the kings of England decided to gather together in one place all of those who had brilliant minds and the place that was chosen was London, which eventually became a city. At one time, the top people of each kingdom, who were the people I mentioned, they were the only people to be involved in the practice and study of science, even before the kids were allowed to be involved. Then more people were invited to the learning of science and these people were the families of the people who were already a part of the learning of science.

When families were invited to the learning of science than the practice and study of science was formed into education and like I said earlier, it was called education when more people became involved with the learning of science. The many family members who were invited to learn science they had to be taught (educated).

When many people began to be taught than the name education was given to the learning of science. This was before many other subjects were added to the program of education. Because there were some many people now involved with the learning of science there had to be a place to teach the many people who were chosen to be a part of this fantastic system. The family members of many kings would go to London only for the purpose of learning science. As the royal families would go there to learn science than other people's talent and skills were discovered. When people were far away from each other then they couldn't find out about the talents and skills of other people. Then the only talents and skills they knew were their own and others who they associated with. But if there is a place where many people get together for a purpose than people can find out about other people's talents and skills.

This can help them to develop a more excellent system than they already had and that was what happened when the royal families got together in one place to learn science. This educational system was put in an orderly fashion concerning the way the royal families would learn science. The Counts that were in charged started the orderly fashion from introduction to advance learning. This is what influenced the Counts to separate the different learnings of science into classes. This allowed for people to learn at their own pace without interfering with others who were learning at a different pace and it also single people out from those who were slow in learning from those who were faster in learning.

This system is the reason why there are different levels of learning classes in schools today, not the colleges, but the schools. Like the special class, which is for kids who have a difficult time learning. Then the C class, which are the average learning kids. Then the B class, which are the kids who are in between and then there is the A class. That was how my elementary school was. That same system was the system that was in the educational system during the time of Count Dracula.

At first, it was only the learning of science that formed and made the educational system that existed in London, but as people began to come to gather to learn science, than the talents and skills of other people in other royal families began to emerge. The different talents and skills of other people is what influenced the Counts to add other forms of learning to the learning of science. When that happened, science wasn't the only subject the royal families could learn in London. When other subjects of learning became another interest than another form of orderly learning was developed and that was the development of different classes.

College was created before school. School was created for the kids and college was created for the adults. Back during the time of Count Dracula, when this system first got started there were times when adults were in the same classroom as the kids because of their learning ability. College was created and used in a little different way than it is used today. College back then was for people who were already advance in the learning of science they just went to college to share what they knew with someone else who had the same advancement in the field of science.

The only reason why the Country of England formed this kind of educational system was to better their Country and keep their Country above other Countries, especially, the Countries that were their enemies. That was the only reason that system was created by the English.

Then the system was slowly used for another purpose and that was to teach others in the royal families about science. Different subjects were added on as people's talents and skills began to flourish. Even the system of receiving a piece of paper as a subject degree to show a person's credentials; started in London England. All the things we learn in schools and colleges today are old, very old. Even the language we speak here in America came from London England.

As different subjects were added to the learning of science, the educational system, the English royal people had created, began to change. The royal people of England became so concerned with the passing down of their intellect, which was only German, they only allowed for their offspring to marry and have kids by other people who were a part of their family.

Even today, the royal families of the English empires only want their kids to marry inside their family, so that no other gene is added to their descendants. In that way, they can make sure that everything the royal family has in their genes is passed down to their future descendants, especially, their intelligence.

The educational system that is in America and the structure of the educational system was created and founded in London England. England has had some amazing people in the history of education. Their intellect gave them the ability to do some amazing things and their intellect gave them the ability to create some amazing things. The Anglo-Saxons, not only advanced their condition of living, but they advanced their ability to learn and to teach others to learn what they have known for years. It is through the learning talent of the English royal family that many other people have had the chance to learn some of the things that have caused many people in the world today to make it to a very high level in many areas of life in this Country. America is only a carbon copy of what England is now and what they were in the past.

The people in London England, who contribute to the development of science, were known as nobleman. A nobleman in England was a man or any man who had some kind of position in the upper class society of England, from the king, to a teacher. A nobleman in England included, a doctor, scientist, lawyer, judge, psychologist, writer, poet and etc. A nobleman was anyone in England that had an education in the upper class society. Any man who was a nobleman in England was called a Count. A Count was a man who had a high rank because of his position and the positions were the ones I mentioned and a few more I didn't mention.

After the educational system was developed in England many things began to change in England. One of the main things that changed in England was the title of people. After the development of the educational system many nobleman were given particular titles and they were known in public by those titles. There titles were based on their profession and their profession was determined by what they studied in college. Back during the time of Count Dracula many nobleman had different professional titles. When the educational system started, the length of time to get a specific degree wasn't as long as it is today.

For that reason, many noblemen had several degrees at once and not only that, but to get an education back than was much easier.

Most noblemen back than would get several degrees in fields that were connected to each other and that is something that many people do today. If a person gets a degree in psychology for instance, than they decide to get a masters, they would get a masters in a degree that is connected to psychology; like sociology because both sciences deals with people's behavior. A nobleman receiving several degrees was very popular and something that was done by just about everyone who went to college to get a college degree. There are very few people today who get two degrees let alone one degree. Most people who are graduates have one degree and a few people have two degrees.

The system of degrees was a little different back then compared to the system of degrees today. The system of degrees back than were on the same level or order. Back than regardless to how many degrees a person received all their degrees were on the same level, which means one wasn't higher than the other. Now, the system of degrees is higher than each other.

For an example, a Bachelor Degree is lower than a Master's Degree and a Master's Degree is lower than a Ph.D. All three degrees are on different levels. There are also some other degrees that are in between those degrees that I didn't mention, but the only ones I know about are the ones I just mentioned.

The level of degrees didn't start until decades later and the level of degrees started in London England. When learning first began it was just in the acknowledgement of learning and not in the acknowledgement of college degrees. The interest of learning was genetic science because genetic science was the science that would teach a person about the things they were most interested in, which was another human being. But as time pressed forward in the advancement of learning than social science became another focus of interest among the educated class of people. Many kings in the different kingdoms were more interested in the social sciences because it helped them to learn the character of their opposing enemies and not only that, but it helped them to determine their character of defense.

The people who became interested in the social sciences other than the king were people who were in charge of the military whose job was to protect the kingdom. They would use that form of science to figure out their opposing opponents on the battle field and off the battle field to try to determine their every move, so they wouldn't be defeated in battle as they fought the other kingdom that were their enemy. The people who also became interested in the social sciences were people who had a very strong interest in the behavior of other people and that kind of science was the excellent study for that kind of focus because it was design to teach a person the motive of other people on a professional level.

The transfer of interest concerning the fields of education took a dramatic turn. When that happened people were still interested in the sciences because social science was considered as a science, but it was a different kind of science that people of science were used to. The science that most scientists were used to was the biological sciences that deal only with the study of life and living organisms. Matter of fact the biological sciences were the first sciences that were studied and practiced by scientists.

Even when social sciences didn't become a form of scientific study to scientists, it was still a form of study, but on a social level and because the social sciences were a form of study that was done on a social level, it wasn't considered as a science of study and practice because the study wasn't a focus study.

To most people, if what is studied is a focus than that is what people consider as important and worthwhile to spent their occupied time on. Although, social science was the first form of science because people first started socializing with each other before they did anything else, scientist didn't focus on it as a practice of study. The reason why they didn't see it as a practice of study is because they didn't spend any occupied time on the practice. The practice of social science at one time was only done through socialization, which is when one person or group of people socializes with each other.

So social science was always a form of study, but done through a social network. Back when science was the main focus in England, the only sciences that were considered as a science was the sciences that occupied a person's time privately, which made the science they studied a focused priority.

Social science wasn't considered as a focused priority because it was a study that didn't require a time for private study, but it was a science that was known, but through a different environment. The environment can determine how important a person view something. The environment that social science was learned was an environment that doesn't require complete focus, which is most of the time done in a private environment. Because social science was always learned through a social environment it was always viewed as a social learning rather than a social science.

Social science became viewed as a scientific study when people who observed other people, began to focus on the pattern of thinking a person had, as their behavior was being studied because than people realized that the person's mind had everything to do with the person's behavior. When social science wasn't viewed as a scientific study method, scientists thought that the study of a person was only done through their behavior and the mind was ignored. Behavior isn't what makes the social science a science because behavior is something that is more observed than studied. The mind is the part of a person's behavior that is studied because the mind is something that causes something else to happen, which is the person's behavior.

Something a person learns every day through something they do every day is considered as non-important, so it is not viewed as the same as something else. This is an example, if you are a reader and you read a lot in private, your reading isn't important as if you were reading to pass an exam or if you were reading to keep up with the a teacher in a class you are taking. So because of that, the private reading you do is viewed by you as different from the reading you do for a class you are taking. One form of reading to you is more important than the other, but both offer the same form of study or can offer the same form of study.

Social science and biological science offers the same adaption, which is learning. A person is able to learn from the both of them, but the way the learning happens, one science is considered as more important than the other science, although, both are equally important because they both requires a person to learn. For a long time, social science wasn't considered to English scientists as a science because social science offers learning that isn't important because of how it was learned, rather than the way that it should have been learned, which is through the study of the mind.

The mind is studied more accurately through the things a person says, rather than through their behavior because a person's behavior is determined by the way they think and the way a person thinks is determined by what you hear them say.

I heard a psychologist say on television one day that she doesn't determine a person's behavior by how they look, she determines their behavior by what she hear them say. The way a person learns social science is the reason why earlier scientists didn't view social science as a science because they didn't view it as important. They thought a person could get more learning from biological science than social science.

When social science was added to the study of science many noblemen became just as interested in this kind of science then the science they had studied and practiced previously. For a long time in England, there was only one scientific study and that was biological science. Social science became a focus to scientists when scientists had a desire to mentally manipulate their subjects, which eventually became other human beings. When science was at its early stage of existence in England; science was only studied and practiced independently because there weren't any species involved with the studies the scientist would perform, but species were used in the study of science in many earlier civilizations. During that time, science was used to study different formulas only for the purpose of creating new formulas and learning about the already existing formulas.

Science back during that time was used more to create a better way of survival. Science was used in England to advance the things that people would need to survive and make life better. The things that science was used for didn't influence scientists to become interested and focused on people. Once science was used on people by scientists in England, then titles were given too many Counts. The ideal emerge to use science on people when many different people from different royal families were brought together for the purpose of learning science. The ideal to use science on people was thought of when many intelligent people were brought together in one place to learn science. Titles and degrees came around the same time.

When scientists started using other people as study subjects than the use of social science became very important. Some studies required manipulation and other studies didn't require manipulation.

When people began to be used for scientific study then titles were given to Counts according to their profession. Counts became professionals when their experience in science was really seen through the way they were able to help other people through the practice of science. Sometimes a person's talent and skill can be seen and recognized better in one area of practice than in another area of practice.

The talents and skills of scientists wasn't actually seen and recognized until they began to receive many compliments for their work. The things Counts did for people put them on a different level of respect.

People always had respect for them because of the different kind of intellect they had from other people, but when they were able to use their intellect to help and save people from their health burdens than their respect from people went over the top. This arrangement between the scientist and another person is what influenced the world of science to create different titles by what they practiced and what they practice is what became their profession. When people were used as study subjects that was when scientists were separated by what they did to other people.

Their separation is what also created their titles. Once scientists were separated than the way to learning the sciences was separated. Once the learning of science was separated, then credentials were created to identify each specific scientist. The credentials were given after the completion of particular classes a person had to take that would qualify them to participate in a particular scientific practice. These credentials are known today as college degrees and they were also known as that back during this time in scientific history.

Degrees created titles and titles created different professions. All the professions were held by noblemen who were called Counts. Most Counts were into the scientific study that eventually became known as the medical profession. The scientific study was eventually changed into the medical field. After that happened, than social science was very important. Matter of fact, social science was jumped up into the top science of study. Because it was important how a medical professional would handle their study subject, which eventually became known as patients. When just about every scientist began to have a direct connection to people they had to practice on two things; the patient and the health problem the patient was having.

To get a better understanding of the patience health problem, sometime, it required a psychological practice. In every medical major today, taking a psychology course or two is a requirement because the only thing a person in the medical field deals with are people. Sometimes a person in the medical field can deal with a patient better if they are able to examine their mind at the same time they are examining their health problem. Even today, people in the medical field have two responsibilities; the mind of the patient and the patient themselves. In the same way, when people began to be a part of the scientific study than the scientists had to learn the mentally of the person and in most cases, they had to learn the mentally of the person to determine what was wrong with the person's health condition and that is the same situation that people face who are in the medical field today.

So for that reason, the science that scientists have ignored for years in England became the forefront in the medical field. The Counts were some amazing people. They were the people who were involved in the scientific world before they received the name Count.

In the earlier times of science they were called scientists, but when titles were added to identify the person's science Profession, the name Count was given to those people as a royal nick name, but there professional name was given according to what the Count practiced. The Counts were the professional people who were responsible for the entire structure of the educational system, so they are the people who are responsible for the educational system we have today. The Dukes and the Marquises were also professional people, but their profession was a social profession rather than a science profession. They were the lawyers, teachers, judges, writers, poets, musicians and etc. Once people came together in London England to learn science and many other talents and skills were discovered by other people whose interest was science, than the Counts were the people in the system who arranged the learning environment to the way the learning environment ended up today in the form of schools and colleges.

The Counts were the professional people that received the most respect among the regular people and also the professional people.

They were respected because of the different things they were able to do that many other professional people weren't capable of doing. At one time, there were only a few of them compared to how many other people there were in the other professions. Counts had the intellect they had because of the way they were allowed to become involved in science at a very young age by their adult parents. Their advanced environment caused their thinking process to advance, which produced thoughts that were equal to the adults who were in the same practice they became involved in as kids.

The way they were raised influenced their royal family members who were their parents to preserve them for the purpose of science. This wasn't an accident or a coincidence it was something that was very carefully planned. This was a way to keep the practice of science active and alive since science was extremely important to the betterment of humanity. It was also a way to keep an intellectual person available to the royal family, especially, to the king and queen of the kingdom. Other kids from other parts of the royal family whose parents weren't involved in science, they were able to be the normal kids that every kid wants to be.

89

Those kids were allowed to be kids. They were the adult who eventually became a part of science after a place was created in London England by the Counts to learn and practice science.

The Counts were the men who were responsible for the entire structure of the kingdoms that existed in the Country of England. Each royal family had their own Counts. Just like each royal family had their own Dukes and Marquises. Each royal family had the same kind of people they were just from a different royal family. Take a family today, some parts of the family are different from other parts of the family, but they are all related. One part of the family   may have educated people and another part of the family may have people who drink a lot; another part of the family may have people who are good in building things, but they are all related.

In every family, people are able to do something different from people who are in another part of their family, but they are all related. The reason why that happens is because whatever it is that a particular part of a family does, most likely their kids pick up the same things and if a particular part of a family have something special, they will see to it that their kids will end up with it, so they can keep that part of the family active and alive. That's what the English people always did to keep certain talents and skills within that part of the family, but they were all royal and related, regardless, to what they could do. The Counts were always from a scientific part of the royal family that's why all of them were scientists.

Even today, a person who is a doctor, they may have been raised different from the rest of the kids who are a part of their family and the reason why I know that is because I have a first cousin who ended up being a doctor and her parents were extremely protective over her. She didn't play as a kid like we did. She was always serious. If she played with us, it was when we were doing so kind of play that would influence us to use our minds, than she would play with us, but other than that she didn't play with us. Look what she has become, an M.D. and to this day she doesn't socialize with any of her first cousins. She is a loner, that's the way her parents raised her, so that is a form of preservation.

That's the same kind of preservation the part of the royal family had that the Count belonged to, so he was completely different from the way the other kids were in the same royal family.

Every parent wants their kid to be successful and the level of success they want for their kid will be determined on how much success they had as adults. A parent can become extreme with the preparation of the success of their kid, if they have had an extremely successful career themselves and sometimes it is nothing wrong with that. That's how each Counts parents were and that was the reason why they were always out front and because they were out front, they were the people who everyone in the royal family would depend on to straighten things out for the kingdom; if the kingdom had a problem.

When a person needs advice they will most likely go to someone who is higher in intellect, if they know someone who has a higher intelligence because that is the person they think could help them by giving them the advice they need. Most people would respond that way if they have a problem that needs solving. That's what the Counts experienced from people on a regular basis. The Counts were extraordinary people and they were able to do some amazing things and they were the people who added a lot to the royal family and that was how they added to the kingdom they belonged to.

Dracula was a Count in London England. He was a very brilliant man. He was a man who had several high positions, because he had several college degrees. His positions caused him to have several credentials. So in London, he was allowed to do several practices. But his specialty was science and medicine with a back ground in psychology. Count Dracula was a nobleman who existed in the 15th century. His main focus was science dealing with human genetics. He was a scientist who dealt with the study of sperm and egg cells.

Count Dracula took the study of science back to its original origin. He was very well respected just like many other Counts before him. It wasn't unusual for a Count to be admired and recognized by other people. That was something that was normal to many other Counts. Back during the time of Count Dracula, many educated people had many different interests in the world of education. Most of the educated people during this time had more of an interest in the social sciences than the medical sciences, which was called in earlier times the sciences. The science in earlier time had a completely different platform. Science was narrowed down to one specific form of science and that was biological science.

The talents and skills of different people offered the existence of other sciences, which began to merge with the more popular, main and oldest science. In the scientific world, in earlier times, there was only one specific form of science and that was the science that all scientists would study, but during the time of Count Dracula all of that changed.

Educated people were learning other sciences that became connected the main science because the other sciences would help the medical professions understand and deal with patients better. Social science is the science that became the main science because more people had the intellect to tackle that kind of science than the medical science. Even today, the science that is the hardest is medical science and it is the science that people are afraid to tackle. In college today, the hardest major to study is anything that is in the medical field of study, so for that reason, many people don't have enough nerve to tackle that kind of major. There are fewer students in medical school than in any other school because there is a much higher commitment in the medical major than in any other major.

Back in the 15th century, the only people who would have the nerve to study in the medical field were the offspring's of the Counts.

Back during this time in the history of education, there was only a certain group of people in each royal family who would make the medical field as their focus of study. Every Count had a higher intellect than everyone else who were involved in some kind of educational program. Even today in college, there are programs that have the brightest college students and if a person's learning capacity isn't high enough than they wouldn't have a change of passing.

There are even some colleges that are geared for the specially talented and you have to take a test that is unbelievably hard to see if you have a high enough IQ to enter and the tuition is ridiculous.

This college system was similar to the college system in the 15th century, but for one program. In the colleges, where a person had to take a test to enter and become a student, all the programs are hard. The ideal to get that kind of college system started from London England when the only people who were able to study and practice the hardest science in college were the offspring's of the Count who were intellectually trained to take on that kind of educational study. Before the educational system started, the kids of Counts would only practice science in the privacy of their parent's homes, but when schools and colleges were created than two places of study existed for the brilliant kids of the royal family.

They were the only kids who would make it in the field of science in England for a long time. There are many people in college today and there are many people who have gone to college who wish they could major in more college subject than what they did. There are many people who graduated from college who wish they could have received several degrees in college.

If you do a survey with people who have graduated from college and ask them if they are satisfied with the degree they have, they will probably make a statement like, I am satisfied with my major, but I wish I could have gotten another degree or two. Most people who have graduated from college wish they could have gotten several degrees other than the one they have. Some people have several degrees; I was listening to this one lady, one night on television that had five different degrees and they were all in the social science field. She had two Bachelors, two Masters and one PH.D. If most people had their choice concerning college they would get several degrees if they could and that was something that was normal for educated people back during the time of Count Dracula, but something that isn't normal today.

It all depends on what your major is and the kind of job you have, which will determine if you are able to use two degrees.

If a person learns and knows the things they studied and they have two degrees and they have a job that ties into both of their degrees, than the experience they received in one program can help and increase their experience in the other program they studied. That was the intellectual talent and skill Count Dracula had. Although, Count Dracula had several degrees he only had two kinds of educational experience. If you would take several classes in the field of psychology or any other field, you will study the same thing as you take different classes. So the things you study in introduction to psychology are the same things you will study in abnormal psychology. You only repeat what you are studying unless you are taking a different course other than psychology courses.

Count Dracula had several degrees, but they were degrees in the medical field and one degree in psychology, so although he had several degrees, he only had two educational experiences. But he used the two educational experiences to help and increase each other and the only way a person can do that is to remember the things they studied in college, which is something that a lot or I will say most people aren't able to do, but Count Dracula was one of those people who was able to do that.

Medicine is what birth the existence of the medical field and science is what birth the existence of medicine. So science influenced medicine and medicine influenced the medical field and the medical field influenced the other sciences that are now a part of the medical field, when the medical field started using people as subjects of study. In the 15th century, everyone who practiced medicine practiced other sciences, but everyone who practiced the other science didn't practice medicine. That's how it is today. I am trying to show you that England was the place where all of our education started. In college today, the people whose major is medical science, they have to take other sciences a part from the science of medicine and most of those sciences are social sciences. But the people whose major is another major other than medicine they don't have to take any medical classes unless they want to. That's the way it was in England in the 15th century.

Most people were able to get several degrees because of two factors. One is; they were so brilliant that they were very important to all of those who were in authority. The second reason was because their relatives were people who were highly respected and that was just about everyone in the royal families. In some areas in the United States, people who attend college experience that kind of favoritism from colleges, but in secret.

Back than that was done it the open and no one could do anything about it. There were many families in England who were rich and wealthy, but they weren't royal. Those were the people who had to pay for their kid's tuition, but if their kid had a talent and skill for learning science than the kid had a pass. Back then people who were able to learn any kind of science were well respected just like if a person would major in mathematics today. They would be respected by people because the first thing people would think about them is they are intelligent.

Count Dracula was respected through the ability he had for using one educational experience to support the other educational experience he had. He could use his experience in psychology to manipulate a person's mind to control the person's behavior throughout the entire secession.

There weren't many then and there aren't many now in the medical field that can do that. The only way a person can take what they learned and use it to control a person's behavior is to know by memory everything they studied in college or studied period in the field of study they are interested in.

Dracula had the same interest as the ancient Africans in the area of science. One of the species Dracula created was the vampire. They were a species that were brought forth from the sperm cell of a bat and the egg of a woman. Count Dracula received permission to do that kind of experiment from the king.

The purpose of the experiment was to create a super human race that would benefit the kingdom that Count Dracula belonged too, so that his kingdom could defeat other kingdoms in battle and defend themselves against other kingdoms. Count Dracula was a mad man, but his madness was completely separated from his intellect of genius. Count Dracula was selected to receive the degrees he had because there was a long list of professional people in his genealogical family background.

Back during that time, the people who were professional, they came from an educated family. The people who didn't come from an educational background weren't allowed to receive an education unless it was something seen about a person that would add to the study of science and education, than it was an exception.

Some professional people looked up the work of other people in the past that had the same profession to see if there is something they did that would help advance their practice. Most people in the field of medicine do a lot of research on other people who were in the same practice as they are. All doctors do that and that has helped many doctors to become better in their area of work. Just like in our time, in past times, there have been some professional people who have done some amazing things. So in the past, there were some brilliant people just like there are now and if people were able to get information about the work they did and the things they have accomplished, they could add on to what they were doing at the present time and what they plan to do in the future.

That was something that Count Dracula did. The people he was most interested were the ancient Africans because all of what he did and his ancestors did, were discovered through the information they received about the scientific studies of people in Africa in ancient times. The ancient Africans spent most of their studies in the scientific world. They spent a lot of time studying and practicing science. They were interested in the merging together of a sperm and and an egg cells. Not just the sperm and egg cells of the same species, but of different species.

They were interested in the creation from two different species and that is why there are many different dogs, cats, birds and many different other animals; it was because of the kind of scientific practice the ancient Africans did and many people in the world of science copies what they did and Count Dracula was one of those people.

Every scientist has their own creation in which they treasure and think very highly of. Count Dracula's scientific practice by way of the medical field gave him the ability to create a species that was superior in strength than a regular human. Count Dracula got involved with this kind of practiced to impress the king of the kingdom he belonged to. Sometime a scientist had to get permission from his king to do certain practices, if they didn't comply than they were killed. Dracula got permission to perform the practice he did and he used the practice to create another species that took on human form. This species was called the vampire and the reason why they were called the vampire was because of the vamps in their teeth, which were something that was new to the human race. Ire because those teeth would stand hire than the rest of the teeth.

Count Dracula received permission from his king to create such a species for the protection of the kingdom against other Countries who were their enemy.

Those species were planned by the king to be used in the military or used to help his military fight against any kingdom they were up against and that's the reason why Count Dracula was given permission to create such a species.

England's main enemy during that time was parts of Germany, which was a Country that was stronger than England during the time of Count Dracula. There are some brilliant people who have a very high intellect, but they are psychologically unfit for socialization. They are very brilliant, but there is a very dark side to them and another person couldn't be trusted alone with them. They have a sense of logic, but it has a short limit. That means they are only able to control it when they are in an environment that taps in and uses the brilliant side of their intellect.

When this kind of mental process happens than at that moment their dark side is undetected because their brilliant side over rides it. The brilliant side becomes the master when they are in a scientific environment and the dark side, I mean very dark side, becomes the slave because their dark side isn't allowed to interfere with the brilliant side that is at work at that particular time. We all experience that, but on a much different level than Count Dracula because most of us don't have a side as dark as Count Dracula.

This is an example of the mental process I just talked about concerning Count Dracula that we all experience, but on a much lower level. Say you were are at work and an another employee did something to you that got you very upset and you wanted to confront them about what they did to you, but the environment, your work place, is what influenced the logical side of your intellect to control the dark side of your intellect and the dark side of your intellect is what you want to actually do to that person.

But because of the environment, the logical side becomes the master and the dark side becomes the slave because the logical side is influencing the dark side to decrease in influence. So it doesn't take that much control to do the opposite from what your dark side wants you to do because the logical side is much stronger. Now say for instance, if the same employee did the same thing to you a long way from the job and after they did it, they say to you come on let's fight and in the same way, you refused, but you wanted to fight.

The reason why you refused is because again your logical side is stronger than your dark side. So you controlled how you responded to the situation. If a person thinks about doing something bad then they have a dark side. Some of us have darker sides than others.

In the case of Count Dracula, it was his brilliant intellect that controlled his dark side, not himself. For an example, Ted Bundy, he was smart, but not brilliant. For that reason, he would try to kidnap a girl in broad daylight in front of other people. His smart intelligence wasn't strong enough to control his dark side because if it was than he would have committed all of his crimes when his intellect would tell him the correct time to do them, but his intellect couldn't tell him that because his dark side was in control of his intellect, so it was him. If a person does something they want to do than it is that person. If a person does something they don't want to do and they do it any way than it is the person's intellect.

When Count Dracula was in a scientific environment there were probably many times he wanted to harm someone who worked with him, but he refused to do it because of the interest in his environment, so it was his intelligence that stopped him because working was something he didn't want to do at the time, but he did it anyway. Because of his brilliance, his intelligence was in control of his dark side. In our case, it is logic that is stronger than our dark side, not our intelligence.

So it is us who refuse to do what our dark side will tell us to do. Intellect comes from the mind and logic comes from the heart.

The mind is not us our hearts is us. Most of the time, when a person is as dark as Count Dracula was and they aren't brilliant like he was, than they can't control the dark side of their character. So they do abnormal things during the times when they shouldn't. That's how Count Dracula was able to continue in his profession, although, he was a mad man.

Back during the time of Count Dracula, people who had a very unusual intellect when it had to do with learning, they were the people who were selected to the world of science and that was something the ancient Africans did. So London and ancient Africa had the same kind of method of recruitment in adding people to the study of science. Back during the time of ancient Africa and London, during the time of Count Dracula, any learning a person did under the power of the king that contribute to the function of society was considered as science. Today, science is separate from many other kinds of study, but back then the study a person did had everything to do with science.

In the Dracula movies, if you can remember, Dracula was the master vampire. He was the person who started the vampire species by biting people on the neck, who eventually turned into a vampire. The vampires were afraid of him, so they respected him. In the movie, the vampire had extraordinary strength. Dracula slept in a coffin and at night he went out to hunt for his prey.

The only way you could kill him was by driving a stake through his heart. Dracula couldn't view the sight of a cross. In the movie, Dracula wore a suit with a cape and sometimes he would turn into a bat. He had telepathic power to influence his victims to come to him so he could bit them and all of them were women. If you can remember, in the first Dracula movies many people weren't bitten. All of this was fiction, but there was something true behind the fiction. I will repeat the last paragraph and explain it as well so try to follow along.

Dracula was the master vampire: Which means: Count Dracula was the man who started the vampire species through his many kinds of experiments.

Out of all of his experiments, that was the experiment he had the most success, so that was the experiment he was recognized for, but the other experiments he didn't receive recognition for. In the experiment that Count Dracula had success in, he was considered as a master because he was an expert in that kind of experiment.

In the world of science, there have been many different experiments for a long time. Some scientists were much better at one particular experiment than the other. Some experiments are harder than others, but all of them are very hard to execute with a precision of competence. All scientists are talented and skillful because if they weren't then their ability to exist in the science world would be just a passing phase. Whenever there is a scientist who has enough skill to perform; just the basics, than most of the time their ability to keep up with the processes of learning that comes with the work is seen and notice at the first stage of practice.

There is a certain skill that a scientist have that many other people don't have and sometimes the only way to see how different they are from regular people is to spent the amount of personal time it takes to see the intellectual side of that person's character. All scientists have their good days and their bad days.

All scientists have their good seasons and their bad seasons. The work they do in their good season is the work that is most of the time used by the people who govern them.

Most scientists today and also in the time of Count Dracula, don't work for themselves, but they learn a lot from the work they perform. Scientists have always been people who work for other people who also have an unusual intellect and character. When two people or two groups of people are brought together for a purpose, then the purpose is always for the king, emperor, minister or president of the Country the scientist lives in.

A leader or government; depending on the times of the world have always put their trust in the intellect of certain person. People who they know can help them accomplish important things to benefit their Country. The leaders of a Country have never been responsible for the advancement of the Country they lead, it was always people who had the skills that are needed to perform the task that leaders have complete obligation to and that is the advancement of the Country.

In the early years of science, the scientist or scientists would report his work directly to the king because during that time the Country the scientist was doing work for actually belonged to the king.

The Country was actually his property just like the castle was his property. The Country was his property because it was owned by his father or grandfather and in most cases, the Country was owned by both in the past.

Once the Country became divided into many different regions then the king needed help governing his kingdom. When the Country became divided, the things that happened inside the kings Country, the king was able to monitor on his own because what was going on in his Country was at his reach. Although, the Country was extremely big, the king was able to keep up with everything that was done for the purpose of his Country.

But when his Country became divided because of the things that were going on in different part of his Country, which were the same things that he was able to monitor at one time himself, than the king had to depend on other people who were a part of his regiment by choice, to do the same kind of monitoring he had done for years when everything was at his reach.

The people who the king would assign to monitor the parts of his kingdom that he couldn't monitor his self were always military leaders: A military man or a group of military men who were responsible for a large number of soldiers. They were the men the king would chose to govern the part of his Country that he couldn't govern himself. This new system, which is the same system the government uses today, in all Countries, was a system that was more than effective enough to keep up with all of the brilliant people who would work for the king for the purpose of his Country.

The work they did was only design to help the Country grow for the better in any way possible. When the king was able to monitor himself, the brilliant people who worked for him, this was at the very early time in science. At the early time in science, the only people who were recognized for their brilliance were people who were a part of the royal family and I didn't mention this earlier, but the royal family consisted of everyone who was related to the king.

That's why the king was able to keep up with all of the people who were brilliant in intellect. There were many other brilliant people who slowly began to merge and they were people who would rent land that was owned by the king and the land they rented from the king was far away from where the king lived, but the region belonged to the king. As many other brilliant people began to merge in a faraway area of the king's territory, the king wanted to keep up with the things they did, but had a hard time doing so himself, so he had to send people he trusted and they were always the men who were in charge of a particular part of his army.

Ever since there were a large number of people the owner of a Country had to govern, there has always been a group of people who were close to the king and they were the people who the king trusted with his life and they were the top military soldiers, who eventually, were given ranked positions by the king. There has always been a strange bond between these kinds of men and the king. A bond that would make the king and the top soldier form a solid friendship that couldn't be broken.

At the earlier years of science in England, the king would choose those kinds of men to monitor people he could no longer monitor. That was how different parts of government were formed. The isolation of brilliant people in Europe started from the Greeks, but brought to an advance level by the English. The English were the Europeans who thought of a system that would allow for the king to monitor people who were far away from his castle.

It was this earlier time that influence the British to gather together all brilliant people in London England for the purpose of learning science, which was once again how school and college started, especially, college. Later, the same system was created, so once again the king could monitor at first hand the work of those who work for him who were brilliant.

That was the way that kind of system remained and that is the reason why it is that way now. If there was a person who comes up somewhere in the state of Ohio for an example, who had a high intellect, than that person would be monitor unknowingly at first by some government agency, than if they see something in the person that could benefit the Country than they will be approached for membership.

That was the way it was in England in the earlier years of science, but now there is a faster way the government can get to a person like that, but in the early times in England, it was hard for the king to monitor other brilliant people outside of the royal family who lived a long way from the king.

There are different levels of intellect in the world of science, but it doesn't matter how intellectual a scientist is, it won't determine if he is considered as a master scientist. What considers a scientist as a master scientist is his work. His work has to be done without any mistakes along the way and his work has to end up exactly the way he predicted it. Take an architect for an example; he predicts his work before he starts his work and his predictions are made through the blueprint he designs for a particular job.

In the same way, that was what scientist did during the time of Count Dracula and that is the same thing they do today. If everything worked out as planned concerning his predictions without any mistakes, then that scientist was considered as a master scientist. Certain experiments a scientist is better in than others. The experiment a scientist have learned to master is mostly the experiment that he has spent a lot of time on and most like it is probably the hardest experiment.

It is hard for any scientist to merge together two different cells of two different species. Sometimes to be successful it takes a countless exhausting amount of time to get it right. The merging of two different cells is a difficult task to complete. It is a difficult task to complete because the cells of two different species can sometime reject each other and when that happens, instead of the two cells coming together, they will push a part from each other.

In order for a scientist to have success in this kind of experiment the scientist has to study the cells character just like he would study the characters of two people. It's just like a psychologist being in a counseling session with a couple who don't like each other and the counselors job is to bring the two people together, but if the two people continue not to like each other than the counselors will fail at his or her task.

An excellent counselor would probably have to work for a while, but through persistence, the counselor could be successful.

The only way the counselor can be successful is to first examine the couple's character and use their character to determine the problem between the two people that is causing them to be a part rather than coming together. Through the learning of their characters, the counselor will have a better chance to merge the couple's relationship together by merging the two together. One stage helps the other stage.

In the same way, in order for a scientist to have success in merging two different cells together, the scientist has to examine the cells characters. Cells are living organisms that have a character like people and they also survive like people. Every living thing has a character, but the function of their character is different. The characters of living cells are influenced by their source of living. Their source of living is what causes them to live.

The source of living for most cells is a wet environment or a moist environment, which is what the structure of a cell is made of. Whatever is in the cellular environment is what controls the character of the cell. It's the same way with us; our environment can influence our character.

So what is in our environment can determine how we will respond and that's the same way it is for a living cell.

In our environment, there are things that can trigger from us either a good character or a bad character. If we encounter a person who has a character we like than that can influence us to accept that person. The person we encounter may have a good character because of a previous environment the person just left. So the good character of the other person we encounter will have an effect on us.

So instead of rejecting the person we accept the person, but if it is someone you know than most of the time it doesn't matter. That is similar to the way it is between living cells. A cell's character can be determined by the character of the other cell. Cells release chemicals that all other cells can pick up. If a cell encounters a similar cell (someone we know) than the two cells will probably merge together, for what purpose, that determines the chemicals between each cell at the time, which is what we call chemistry. If two people have the same chemistry than   they will probably be a perfect match than a bonding will happen. That's the same way it is for cells.

A perfect and excellent scientist can figure out how to merge two cells together by learning the cells characters just as a perfect and excellent counselor can merge together a disturbed couple, if the counselor has success examining the couple's characters.

Count Dracula was a perfect and excellent counselor of cell character, which was something that other scientist had a very difficult time executing. It was something that was easy for Count Dracula to do. For him it was just like working with the characters of two people. That's why he had permission from the king to perform the kind of practice he performed to create the vampire.

The king knew for sure that Count Dracula was on to something that could make his military the greatest military on the planet at that time and that was something that all kings wanted throughout history for the existence of their kingdom, so their kingdom would remain in their family.

The extreme success that Count Dracula had in that field of research is what made him a master scientist and because of the creature he created, which was the vampire, that's the reason why Count Dracula was the master vampire in the older Count Dracula movies.

He was the person who started the vampire species by biting people on the neck who eventually turned into a vampire: Which means: Count Dracula was such an expert in that kind of experiment that every vampire species came out to be the same way. There was nothing different between them all. Every time Count Dracula would mix together the sperm of a bat and the egg of a woman, he would get the same results every time, a vampire species. Just as Count Dracula would get the same results every time he bit someone in the movie. Count Dracula got better as he kept doing his experiment, which was what it meant when one vampire would bit someone and they would turn into a vampire.

Chimera genetics is a science that a lot of people fail at in the science world. Not just back during the time of Count Dracula, but throughout scientific history. It is a practice that is very difficult to learn. It is more difficult if the scientist is working with two different cells from two different species. That kind of scientific practice is very difficult if the scientist is working with two of the same cells from the same species. When a scientist interferes with the natural pattern of an existing life form, sometimes it is impossible for them to have a successful and accurate result. Most of the time, something goes wrong in the practice.

When a scientist is involved with a practice they are examining through observation, than they are allowing the subjects to preform naturally, which is the way the subjects are supposed to interact with each other. This is an example, say a lady had a husband who can't get her pregnant and she decides to have an artificial insemination, it would be a hundred times harder for her to get pregnant that way than the natural way a woman gets pregnant, which is through sexual intercourse. If there is a doctor who can perform that kind of practice with success than that is a perfect and excellent doctor.

There were many doctors in the past who couldn't perform that kind of practice because it is something that is done by breaking the laws of nature concerning how a pregnancy is supposed to happen, but there have been some doctors who had success in that kind of practice, but not many compared to the number of doctors who went into that kind of practice, but there have been some doctors who had success in that kind of practice, but not many compared to the number of doctors who went into that kind of practice.

If there was a doctor who had success in that kind of practice than there probably were times when they didn't have success. When there is a medical practice that is extremely hard to execute than the doctor who specialize in that practice don't have success every time.

They will have good days and they will have bad days. They will have a good season and they will have a bad season. Any medical practice that is performed artificially and not naturally by a scientist or a doctor is a hard practice to execute correctly. There are many scientific practices that require artificial practice and there are many practices where artificial practice was decided to be used because of the difference in the physical makeup of the two species that were chosen for a specific practice.

For instance, if a scientist wanted to use two different species for interbreeding and there was no way possible for the two different species to have sexual intercourse with each other because both species have a different physical makeup that wouldn't allow for them to have sexual intercourse. Than in that case, an artificial practice has to be used to carry on and complete the practice that a scientist wants to perform.

In this case, it is very difficult, to very difficult, for this kind of practice to be successful, but the scientist who has something in the world of scientific practice that other scientists or most scientists don't have; he might be successful. One time I was watching this medical program and there was something wrong with this patient and all the doctors in the hospital couldn't find out what was wrong with the patient; this one doctor keep on trying and trying and trying, than he finally figured out what was wrong with the patient, it was incredible I will never forget that.

A practice that is very difficult to perform, it takes a doctor or scientist who has a special talent and skill for the practice to cause the practice to be successful. A lot of doctors have a difficult time performing certain medical procedures. Some medical procedures are easy and some are hard. Some scientific procedures are easy and some are hard. All the medical and scientific procedures that require artificial insemination are very difficult to perform correctly.

All forms of artificial insemination are very difficult, even the ones that require the same cells of two of the same species, but the ones that are performed with two different cells from two different species is even more complicated to perform, but the right scientist can perform it with no problem at all. The right and correct scientist for that kind of practice is a scientist who is perfect and excellent at cellular character.

There is a way to merge two different cells together. In order to do that, a scientist has to figure out how to attract a cell or what attracts a cell. If a scientist can create an environment that will attract a cell than he can artificially create a cell character for a specific cell that another cell would be attracted to. When cells are attracted to other cells than a bonding will take place just like if we are attracted to someone than a bonding takes place.

If a person you came in contact with came from a previous environment that made them extremely happy, than their happy character will probably make you happy. For the other person it is not artificial, but for you it is artificial. Why? Because they are actually happy, you are happy because of them

It is the same way with cellular character. If a scientist can create an artificial environment that attracts a certain cell, than put another completely different cell in the same environment that attracted the other cell and then put those two cells together than that will influence both different cells to come together and bond, which would produce fertilization between the two cells, if they are cells that can reproduce because all cells can't reproduce.

This is the part of cellular science that Count Dracula master completely. At the top of his career he was incredible. His highly successful experience in chimera genetics is what made it possible for him to merge together the sperm of a bat and the egg of a woman with no problem at all. He had success every time and the practice went the same way every time. He had good days and good seasons all the time in that specific practice.

He never failed. Just like in the movie, every time Count Dracula or a vampire would bite a person on the neck they changed to a vampire every time.

The vampires where afraid of him so they respected him: Which means: That every time a vampire was born they were properly raised and trained. They were raised and trained for many things, but one thing they learned was to respect the person who created them who was Count Dracula.

Every scientist has a place where they work, which is the same place they keep the things their work created. Most of the time, it is a place that is isolated from the public view. Most of the time, it is a place that is separated from regular society.

This was done for a reason. Sometimes scientists don't want people to know about their work, especially, if their work is harmful to other people. The main reason is that the work a scientist is doing for a particular person, it's the person the scientist is working for who doesn't want other people to know about the scientific research they are responsible for.

Scientists like to have complete control of their scientific environment. They especially like to have control over the things they create. Most scientists are fanatics about maintaining control over whatever is it they have created, especially, if what they create is a living orgasm. Scientists like to learn and know the character of their laboratory subjects. Through the orders of the king, Count Dracula was trying to make a different species for the purpose of satisfying the king.

The King wanted Count Dracula to create a new race of people that could help his already existing army defend his kingdom because at the time there were other powerful kingdoms that were enemies to the kingdom that Count Dracula belong to. That was the first plan of Count Dracula's king. The second plan for creating a new superior race of people was to try to take control of other kingdoms for the purpose of power expansion. Every king back in the 15th century had the desire to expand their kingdom. The more property a king had, the more power a king could receive.

Count Dracula's king had the thought to expand his kingdom and he thought that the scientific practice that Count Dracula learned to master was the key and a way to do what he had a strong desire to do. When a new species is created by two or more species that already exist, the new species will have the genetic make of the other species in which it came from.

One genetic makeup always dominates the other genetic makeup. The genetic makeup that is the dominant makeup is the genetic makeup that controls most of the characters of the new species, but the other characters of the non-dominant genetic makeup are also seen. It's works the same way between a man and a woman who has a child, but on a little different scale.

When a man and a woman have a child, the child is easy to control and teach. Because the child's genetic makeup is already design to fit and adjust to its living habitation, that's why when the fetus is still in the womb of the mother it can respond to the environment that it will eventually become a part of.

It was this young lady I knew one time who had gotten pregnant. When her baby was five months old, the baby would bounce every time she would turn on some music.

Her unborn baby was responding to the music she played and the reason why that happened is because the genetic makeup of the unborn child was designed to adjust to the habitation that her unborn child would become a part of. That's the way it is for all unborn babies. That's the reason why there is so much movement from the unborn baby because they are only reacting and responding to their environment. Some unborn babies can't wait to be born.

Unborn babies become adjusted to their expected environment because the mother is adjusted to the same environment the unborn baby will be a part of. Like I said earlier, cells have characters that are connected to the environment they live in to survive. The cells character is what makes it active and alive, which produces movement. When an unborn baby is active in the mother womb most of it is cellular movement.

Cells are more in control of an unborn baby than the unborn baby itself because cells are forming and are still growing inside the fetus. Cells are the reason why we live. Our entire being is made of cells, so our bodies are only cells. Even the solid parts of our bodies are made up of cells because it is cells that caused the solid parts of our bodies to exist.

Through the umbilical cord, the mother communicates with the fetus without her even knowing it. This communication is done through two pathways; the nervous system and the cell system.

In the fetus, the cells control the nervous system. The cells of the fetus are connected to the cells of the mother through the umbilical cord. Cells constantly go through the umbilical cord from the mother to the fetus and back to the mother again. Through this cellular communication, the fetus can determine what is happening on the outside of the mother womb. The fetus becomes aware of the mothers environment through cellular communication.

The cells of the unborn is already used to the mothers environment and her cells gives information to the cells of the fetus to what is going on in the her environment. So the cells of the fetus help the unborn baby adjusted to the mother's environment before the baby is born. When the baby is born, the baby is adjusted to the environment; it just has to be taught to learn the environment. Because of this, the baby is easy to train.

Take a dog for instance, a dog is hard for people to train because the dog's cells aren't adjusted to our environment, they are adjusted to their environment.

Just like an unborn baby, an unborn estrus (dog) learns the mother's environment through cellular communication, so when the dog is born, it is adjusted to their environment instead of our environment. That's the reason why dogs are hard to train for our environment.

Cells are what cause the brain to think. The cells of the brain are connected to the environment species are a part of and they help the brain think according to the environment it is used to. A dog's environment is in our environment, but it isn't connected to our environment because dogs can't react and respond the way we do to our environment. So a dog's environment is different from our environment.

When dogs are trained right they are more afraid of you than they would be if they aren't properly trained, it's just hard to train them for our environment because of different cell makeup. That's the same way it was for the vampire species, but on a much lower level. The reason why it was on a much lower lever was because the vampire species had two different cellular makeups.

The two genetic makeup of the vampire was the genetic makeup of a bat and the genetic makeup of a human, whereas, the dog only has one genetic makeup. One genetic makeup was more dominant and the other genetic makeup was less dominant. The genetic makeup of the woman was more dominant than the genetic makeup of the bat because the woman was the host. Because the woman was the host, it was her cells, the cells of the vampire species was communicating with, not the cells of a bat.

Because the human cells were more dominant, because the woman was the host, they created an artificial environment for the cells that were less dominant, which only goes back to what I said on page 49, in the first paragraph about an artificial environment. The environment for the human cells was a natural environment, but for the bat cells, it was an artificial environment because it wasn't an environment that matched the habitat of the bat. Through the human cells, the bat cells learned to adjust to an environment they weren't used to.

Similar to what I said at the end of the first paragraph on page 49, which says, if a person you came in contact with came from a previous environment that made them extremely happy than their happy character will probably make you happy.

For the other person it is not artificial, but for you it is artificial. Why? Because they are actually happy, you are happy because of them.

The human cells naturally adjusted to the environment of the woman and the bat cells adjusted to the woman's environment because of the human cells. The human cells were happy, the bat cells were happy because of the human cells. The human cells influenced the bat cells to adjust to the woman's environment. If there are two people who are sharing the same space and one person is dominant and the other person is less dominant, the person who is dominant will have an influence over the person who is less dominant. This all happens because of character.

It is two characters interacting with each other. One character is the leader and the other character is the follower. The character that follows is the character that has to adjust because mostly the person who is the follower isn't used to the things they are influence to do by the person who is dominant.

In the same way, if there are two different genetic makeup of a specific species, than one cell is the leader and the other cell is the follower and that happens because of cellular character. The human cells of the woman influence the cells of the bat to do something they weren't used to doing and that was to adjust to a host they weren't used to. Normally, cells don't have to adjust to a host because the cells are a part of the host because of the same genetic makeup the cells have with the host.

Adjustment for a cell is very important because if it can't adjust than it won't survive. Sometime one person can teach another person how to survive, in the same way, one cell can teach another cell how to survive in an environment the cell don't belong to. This is what happens in genetic engineering. Sometimes cells are influenced by their own family cells, but that doesn't happen that often.

Cell adjustment happens in a very short period of time, regardless, if a cell is influenced or not. Although, the bats cells adjusted to a different environment and became a part of that environment, the character of the bat was seen through the vampire species and that character was the character the bat uses to feed. The bat survives from the blood of other species, so it feeds from the blood of other species and this was one of the characters of the vampire.

The vampire wasn't as hard to train as a dog. The reason why the vampire wasn't hard to train as a dog was because the cells of the bat learn to adjust to the host through the cells that were human. Just as Count Dracula learned the characters of cells he was also able to learn the character of the vampire. Learning cell character was much more advanced than learning the character of the vampire. So what was more advanced for Count Dracula caused him to learn what was less advanced and that will take you back to what I said on pages 7 and 8. Count Dracula had a thinking process that helped him to understand something that was less advanced through something that was more advanced, but both of what he learned was highly advanced. We all have that same kind of thinking process, but on a much lower intelligence.

Learning cellular character prepared his thinking for the learning of vampire character. His learning of cellular character made him very successful in learning the vampire's character to the point of being able to use the host character to influence the guest character. Characters are controlled by genes and genes are controlled by cells because in the cell is where you will find genes. Cells influence genes and genes influence character. The hosted character was the human character and the guest character was the bat character.

What Count Dracula figured out is that the attraction of the characters of cell is the same as the attraction of the characters of behavior. Our behavior comes from cells when cells act the same way they acted when a scientist is able to see the character of the cell, rather than through the behavior of a person. Count Dracula realized that the character of a cell was the same as the character of a person, so he remember all of his practices and the results of his practices, he used what he remembered to learn how to control and manipulate the vampires character. In that way, he was able to properly raise and train the vampire, the same way a mother would train their child.

In the movie, the vampire had extraordinary strength: Which means: The vampire was a strong species in the mind, not in body. In the body, the vampire was no stronger than a regular human, but his mind was different. It was the vampire's state of mind that made it stronger than a regular human. I don't know if you ever worked around people who are mentally ill. But they are stronger than other people who are normal in the mind. Their bodies aren't stronger, but their minds are.

Their minds have such a strong psyche that they can psych themselves up so much in the mind they can have the strength of four people combined that was how the vampire was.

The merging of two different cells to create a new species can have pros and cons. In the case of the vampire, the pros were it was more like a human than a bat, but some of the bat's characters were see in the vampire. The cons were the other side of the vampire that wasn't human. To another scientist, it would have been a difficult experiment because the vampire would have been difficult to handle for another scientist.

Another scientist would have had a difficult time with the vampire because the vampire was a little different in character than a regular human being. They were different because they had a different pattern of thinking. There thinking pattern was different because they were mentally ill. Most of the time that is the result of that kind of experiment, but Count Dracula knew that along with other scientists who did the same kind of experiments. The mind is affected a lot by that kind of experiment because when the fetus is developed their brains are developed first. The brain is the center of the central nervous and the other parts of the nervous system is connected to it after the brain is created.

The mind is affect by that kind of experiment because the brain is the first thing to develop on the fetus and the human cells can't influence the bat cells to adapt to the environment because the environment isn't completely created at that time.

So for that reason, the bat cells that are in the brain, as the brain is being created; they take part in the creation of the brain, but once the brain is created than the human cells become the host.

Is just like if you would start a job and the job you are working on requires a lot of heavy parts, you will probably have to get someone to help you carry the parts in the building, but when you get the parts in the building then there is machinery in the building that can help you carry the heavy parts to where you work, so than you don't need the other person any more.

That's how it is between two different cells that share the same host. The cells that are the helper are the bat cells and the cells that needed help were the human cells. Once the brain skeleton is created (one employee helping the other employee, bring the heavy parts in the building) than the human cells don't need assistance from the bat cells, but the bats cells have already made a place in the brain (the employee who helped the other employee is in the building).

The human cells used the bat cells to assist them because at the beginning there aren't enough human cells to do the job because the human cell didn't merge with another human cell, it merged with a bat cell, which is a foreigner. So the human cells have to use whatever cells are available to start the job.

Once the skeletal part of the brain is developed, than the human cells don't need the bat cells anymore, so because the bat cells are the guest cells they   are   influenced by the human cells. It just like if a person had a building business and one day they didn't have no workers to help them, than they decide to go to a place where guy hang out in the morning hoping someone would pick them up for work.

The man goes to that place and pick up ten guys to help him. When they begin to help him they have a little independence from the man, than after they get things set up, then the man begins to influence the men to do certain thing that relates to the job. That's how it is between two different cells at the beginning of the creation of a species. At the beginning, they work together as an equal, but when the first thing is created, one group of cells becomes the influencer and the other group of cells becomes the influenced.

When the human cells and the bats cells came together to create the first thing, which is the brain, before the human cells became the influencer, the bats cell had already found a place in the brain and caused the thinking of the vampire to be different from the thinking of a normal human being. The mind is a powerful thing. It can cause a person to do something a person won't normally do.

If the brain thinks different from the way the brain normally thinks, than the person will do something another normally thinking person won't do or can't do. The vampire's thinking was different from the normal thinking of a normal person and it caused the vampire to have extraordinary strength.

Count Dracula knew every time that would happen before he completed the vampire experiment. He had a blue print just like an architect makes a blue print to predict his work and Count Dracula predicted his work and his work happened the way he predicted it and that is connected to what I said on page 46, in the first paragraph.

He slept in a coffin and at night he went out to hunt for his prey: Which means: Back during the time of Count Dracula, the only person who was buried in a coffin was a nobleman. Other people were buried in wooden boxes.

The coffin only symbolized Count Dracula's statue in society and it also revealed the purpose of his experiments and that was to bring death to people. The people Count Dracula would gather up as prey for his creation; were people who used to spend some of their time out at night, but in another kingdom.

During the night was when Count Dracula would order some people to go out and gather up people for his creation. Count Dracula's creation strived and lived off of blood, not meat, just as the bat does.

Ever since there have been groups of people living together, people have been separated according to their statue in the world. Today, there are five classes of people; the upper class, the upper middle, lower middle, working class and the poor, but in the 15th century England and in many other parts of the world during that time, there were only two classes of people; the upper class and the poor. The upper class people lived completely different from the poor and that is the way it is today. There were many things the upper class people did that the poor people were able to do. A person was placed in their social class according to how much money they had and that's the way it is today. The more money a person has will determine the social class they will be in.

In England in the 15th century, the upper class lived different than the poor. They lived different because the upper class was able to do things in society that the poor weren't able to do. The upper class was able to do the things they did because of the amount of money they had. In the world, people have always needed money to do the things they wanted to do, especially, when it had to do with survival. Today and even back than a person's social class can be determined by other people by what that person does.

The upper class and the poor do the same things as they live in the world among each other, but because of the financial situation between the two, the upper class people do things in a different way from the poor. Back during this time, people traveled from one place to another, which is something that all people did back than; regardless, of their social class. Back then all people wore clothes. The way they did those things had everything to do with the amount of money they had.

The amount of money people have will determine what is available to them. When people have money they can influence people who don't have money to do things for them. Money has been the means and the way people could influence another groups of people to become their slaves, servants or helpers and it doesn't matter how many people are being used by the person who has the money to hire them.

Just like today, back than the upper class would hire people who didn't have money, so they could have money to survive. The way people became rich or wealth back during the time of Count Dracula was different from the way it is now.

Back during the time of Count Dracula, people became rich or wealth from the things they owned, especially, land. Land was the main thing that made people rich and wealth. Land was used by the rich and wealth to bring the people under their power that was under them.

As a result of that, the lower people were forced to become a part of a system of exchanged the Greeks developed, but didn't start. When someone develops something that doesn't mean they started it. In most cases, what a person has developed they got from the ideal and work of someone else. What they did was is they brought it to another level or a higher level, which made the system more reliable and affective.

The system the Greeks started, in which the English developed during the time of Count Dracula, was the purchasing of people through the use of money. Back during this time and even now, the wealthy people were the people who would create coins and placed them in society by the people they used to work for them for a day's pay.

That was what the Greeks did and that was what the English did, but on a different and higher level. Back during this time, the wealthy people were the people who controlled things and the rich supported the wealthy at what they did, but the both of them were considered as the upper class because both groups were able to do the same things in their living practices.

When people would hire other people, the people who did the hiring became richer or wealthier. The reason why is because the people who were hired, they would help the person who hired them at something the person who hired them couldn't do on their own, which caused them to make more money. This is an example, using modern terms that can be applied back then.

Take a place that makes cell phones for an example, if the people don't work, who works for them, than cell phones aren't made and if cell phones aren't made, than the person who owns the business won't make money. So the people who work for them will cause them to make more money and   become   richer. That's how the rich and wealthy became richer and wealthier through the people they had working for them.

During the time of Count Dracula, the people who were rich were relative of the people who were wealthy and the rich people who weren't related to the wealthy were rich because at one time they probably had something to do with the wealthy. An example of that is the military soldier, the Knight. He was given privileges from the king that caused him to become rich.

Because of money, the rich and the wealthy would do something the poor couldn't do and that was to live a lavish life style. The rich and wealthy hire the poor, not only do things that would help them to make more money, but to help them to live according to their means, which is to help the rich and wealthy live the way they wanted to live. The rich and wealthy people wanted to look different and do things differently than the poor. Not to separate themselves from the poor, but to live in a way that would support their statues in the world. Would a rich or wealthy person live in a gang infested neighbor or would a rich or wealthy person drive in a car long distance to see a relative. No, they will do what supports their statue in the world, which is to live in an upper class neighbor or fly in their private jet to see a relative.

During the time of Count Dracula, the rich and wealthy would do things that would support their statue in the world and that was doing things the poor couldn't do, all the way down to the way the rich and wealthy buried themselves.

The rich and wealthy were buried in coffins and the poor were buried in boxes, if they were buried in something at all. The coffins the rich and wealthy would use for the dead were coffins that were made by people they had hired.

There were some wealthy people who were evil and they would take complete advantage of other people who were much less fortunate. Most wealthy people during the time of Count Dracula had a habit of hanging out with each other during the night. Night was the time when the wealthy would have lavishing parties and most of them were held at night. Count Dracula was one of the people who would participate in night parties and the night parties that he would participate in were the parties that were held by people in his circle. The people who were in his circle were the people who had the same interest as he did and that was the world of science. Because Count Dracula came from a world that influenced night parting and the night life, the night life was what he was used to.

That influenced him to do his dirty work at night concerning his vampire creation. His vampire creation survived from blood and just like the bat, the main time they were active was at night just like the bat is active at night and sleep through the day. Count Dracula chose the night time to go out and gather up people to feed his creation. In reality, there weren't as many vampires as in some of the vampire movies. Matter of fact, in the original movies there weren't many vampires like the later vampire   movies.
Count Dracula chose the night to do his evil work because the night was what he was used to because of his life style.

The only way you could kill him was by driving a stake through his heart. Dracula couldn't view the sight of a cross: Which means: Count Dracula was a very heartless man. He didn't have any feeling for anyone. What drove him to be that way was the dedication he had toward his work. But there were some people he cared about a lot and those people were in his heart and those people were his biological family. Eventually, Count Dracula's whole family was killed by another king from another kingdom. Why? Because the people he gather for his creation were people who came from another king's kingdom and not his own kingdom.

So the king of the kingdom, he gather his prey from, killed everyone in his family and he committed suicide because of that, a stake through his heart. He had nothing to do with God (sight of a cross).

During the time of Count Dracula, it was forbidden for a person to do anything on another king's territory without getting the king's permission. It was forbidden to do anything in the kingdom a person belonged to without getting permission from their king to do so. A person had to get permission by the king if it was something that would or could affect his kingdom. If a person didn't get permission from the king, than the consequences was death and death to the person's family.

During the time of Count Dracula, if a person would do something on the king's territory that would or could affect his kingdom, than that was a heartless person. It is a person who doesn't care about anything. It's just like if a person would kidnap a high government official's kid than that person is heartless because only a person who is heartless would do something like that.

People who have very important jobs are more dedicated to their jobs than other people who are on less important jobs. The more important a job is, the more dedicated they are to their job.

There are some jobs in the world that require complete dedication. There are some jobs that cause a person to be isolated from the company of others. The kind of jobs that require that kind of socialization can have an emotional effect on the person who has that kind of job. People who have very important job that require isolation, they can become emotionally disconnected to other people and if that is the case, the people they only care for are the people who are their immediate family.

When a person reaches that stage of emotional function then they can be a danger to themselves and most of all to other people. If they have to they will violate other people for the purpose of their job because their job is the only thing they care about. They will most definitely harm those who are a benefit to their work, if the benefit is the person. If that is the case, than all rules of logic don't apply.

People who are like this, they mostly likely don't want to do with anything that will remind them of their wrong doings. So their decision to involve themselves with certain environments, are extremely limited and not only their environment, but what they chose to be around. People who do evil don't having anything to do with God because God will bring then face to face with the wronging they have a desire to do. People who are evil, they don't want anything to do with an object or objects that will remind them of God.

That was the way Count Dracula was. There were many people during his time that had a lot to do with God because that was the period in European history that Christianity was at a rise. So many people during the time of Count Dracula would attend church on a regular basis.

Count Dracula was the opposite concerning God. Count Dracula didn't have anything to do with God. He didn't have anything to do with God not just because he was evil, he also didn't have anything to do with God because of his mental condition. Like I said earlier, his mental condition was the reason why he was a mad man and people who have that kind of mentally don't have anything to do with God.

Why? Because to them that is a form of control. People who have the mentally that Count Dracula had, they are people who like to be in control rather than being controlled and have something to do with God is a form of control because it can influence them to reject what they want to do that goes according to their mental principles.

Count Dracula was a person who was used to being in control. Matter of fact, most Counts were used to being in control because they were people who were looked up to by others and if they had additional admiration from people than that increased their level of wanting to be in control.

Count Dracula's need to be in control was far passed the norm, which was the reason why he decided to go on another king's territory without permission. People who do things like that are people who want to be in complete control. Today, Count Dracula would have been labeled as a serial killer. Count Dracula had the same mentally as a serial killer because all serial killer like to be in control and their desire to be in control always reaches far passed the norm, which influences extreme results and Count Dracula's extreme result was when he decided to go on another kings territory without permission.

In the movie, he wore a suit with a cape and sometimes he would turn into a bat: Which means: Back during the time of Count Dracula, a nobleman wore a suit with a cape attached to it. In the movie, don't you remember Count Dracula was four or five hundred years old? Well, four or five hundred years ago was the time period when this happened. Sometimes he would turn into a bat: Which means: Sometime Count Dracula had a taste for blood himself just like his creation and just like a bat does.

Rich and wealthy people now and back during the time of Count Dracula had a distinction to their appearance. They dressed in certain ways. All rich and wealthy men were considered as noblemen because of the position they had in society in which they gained through the money they had access to. During this time in English history, noblemen were always dressed when they were in the public view just like some people of statue today.

Today, there are some people of statue who dress distinctive every time you see them and that was the way noblemen were in England during the time of Count Dracula. A person would never see a noblemen dressed in a regular way. They always would dress in a suit with a cape attached to the back of it. The cape was like a covering for their entire body.

The cape had the same use as a trench coat does today. So a cape was a form of trench coat and it was only worn by prestigious men during the time of Count Dracula and Count Dracula was also prestigious.

There is a time period when a certain dress fashion is in, well four or five hundred years ago was when all noblemen in England would have a cape attached to their suit, which also was the time period when Count Dracula existed.

Just because a person is brilliant that doesn't mean they don't have a mental illness. In the past, there were a lot of brilliant people who were mentally ill and the strange thing about that is they were people who were a part of a prestigious family who may have contributed to the better of mankind.

In the past, there were a lot of people who had high educations and intellects who would do things that other normal people won't do. Sometime the mind can turn against us. When the mind turn against us that is when we will do something that is abnormal. The mind goes against us when the mind doesn't think the way the mind is supposed to think.

There is a reason for that. The thoughts of the mind are a chemical because the thinking of the mind goes through a process to reach the form of thoughts. When there is a malfunction in the thinking process than there is a malfunction in the thoughts that are developed through the brain's thinking.

Thoughts are developed, not created because thoughts already exist before they are formed. Thoughts already exist through thinking. Certain cells are responsible for the brain's thinking. When cells don't agree then they don't work properly together. If there is a group of people who are working together to build something and one person comes to work drunk. The person who is drunk will disrupt the entire order of production. That's the way it is concerning the cells that influences the mind to think.

When there is a cell or cells that aren't working properly it interferes with the normal process of thinking.

It all depends on how many cells there are that are malfunctioning that will determine the severity of the abnormal behavior. The normal cells that control and has everything to do with the person's intellect is more powerful than the cells that are abnormal in functioning. How much power the cells have that controls a person's intellect, over the cells that are abnormal in functioning is determine by the amount of cells between the two groups. If there are more intellectual cells than abnormal cells than the person's intellect can continue to function and that's the reason why you have some brilliant people who are abnormal sometimes in their behavior.

That was the kind of mental environment Count Dracula had in his mind. This kind of mental environment can influence a person to copy the abnormal behavior of someone else. Count Dracula's creation influenced him to participate in the same abnormal behavior they did, which was to feed from blood.

He had telepathic power to influence his victims to come to him so he could bit them and all of them were women: Which means: Count Dracula's interest of study was also psychology. Psychology is the science that studies the mind. Through this form of science, Count Dracula was able to create mental tactics of influence that would gain the trust of other people, especially women. With this trust he would lead women to his place of experimentation were the women would be used as laboratory subjects.

There are many forms of social sciences. In college, a social science major can take many classes in social science. There are also many majors in the social science field. At one time, social science wasn't considered as a science because of the way it was studies. When people began to be the subjects of science then social science had to be treated with respected.

That is when scientist had to adapt that form of science by learning it and also adding their intellectual learning abilities to the science. Social science became interesting and attractive to scientists when the study of social sciences began to take a change in the way social science was use to study the behavior of people.

When social science was used to study the behavior of people through the study of the mind, than scientists became interested because it was the kind of scientific study they were always involved in.

The only difference is they began to study something that was invisible, but the same intellectual practice and focus that scientists have always used towards the study of science, it was now used in the social sciences. Once people became subjects of science then it was mandatory for scientists to use social science in their practices.

Scientists than had to get involved with the research of social science when the mind of a person was the target for their behavior. Why? Because the study of the mind is similar to the study of biological science because in biological science a scientist studies a lot with cells and the minds thinking is influenced and operated by cells.

That's the reason why when the mind became the focus for the study of human behavior, scientists became interested because the same focus a scientist would have toward biological science was the same focus he would have to have toward the study of the mind. That's the reason why scientist became interested in social science after the mind began to be the target of study.

The first people to use social science as a study were called behaviorist. Before the mind became the target for the study of behavior, they didn't consider social science as a science. Matter of fact, it wasn't called social science, it was called behavioral theory.

Scientists were the people who came up with the ideal to study and target the mind as a means for behavior and they began to do so when people became the subject to science. Because one individual was the way a scientist had added people to the study of science is the reason why psychology was the first form of social science. Because it was an individual person a scientist would deal with rather than two or more people, is the reason why psychology was their only focus of study in the social science field for years. They studied the social science that dealt with two or more people, but it wasn't their focus.

So when scientists began to get involve with the study of psychology, psychology became one of their majors along with medical science. Today, medical science only focuses on the handling of patients to improve their physical health, but back during the time of Count Dracula, medical science was more in the form of research to improve people's physical health. Because of that, people back than were used more as laboratory subjects of study rather than medical patients.

So back during the time of Count Dracula, scientists would look at the people they studied and dealt with them similar to the way they would look at a rat they were studying because at that time scientists were looking for solutions to health problems rather than a cure to health problems.

When psychology was mastered by scientists, many scientists used psychology to manipulate their human subjects, especially, if the person was going to be used for an experiment that could bring harm to the person and one of the scientists to use this form of manipulate through psychology was Count Dracula. Count Dracula used this form of manipulation towards women and women only. He used it towards women because women were the only subjects that could be used in the kind of experiment he used to create the vampire.

A lot of people who have majored in psychology don't realize the kind of manipulation they can have on a person, if they were able to understand and see through the mysteries of psychology and all of it is there in the courses a person would take in psychology. It was this show I was watching one day about a group of people who learned the crap game table at casinos. What they did is they created a crap game table in a house they shared and the way the ball went around before it landed on a number was the same way it was at a casino.

They knew for sure that there was a predictable system to that game and they actually figured it out. It took months for them to figure it out, but they did. Once they figured it out than they were able to win when they wanted to and there was nothing the casino could do about it because they use a legal tactic. Because of their tactic it wasn't considered as cheating.

In the same way, if a person could learn to master the stuff they had learned in their psychology courses than they will be surprised how much they can manipulate other people, just as that crew of people learned how to manipulate the crap table. It takes a special mind, not a brilliant mind to do that and Count Dracula had that kind of mind. He used his skills in psychology to manipulate women where he was able to lead them into a situation that they wouldn't have agreed to voluntarily and that was to be a part of an experiment that he was in control of. Through the manipulation he was able to lead them to the place where his experiments were being performed.

If you can remember, in the first Dracula movies many people weren't bitten: Which means: The mistake Count Dracula made was when he went on another king's territory and gather his people up without permission, which brought an end to his experiments because he killed himself by suicide.

Count Dracula didn't use women as laboratory subjects that lived in the same kingdom he did because his king wouldn't have given him permission to do that. So Count Dracula had to use people who lived in another nearby kingdom own by another king. This king was a rival of the king who owned the kingdom that Count Dracula lived in. Back than if a person from one kingdom would violate the rules of another kingdom than that person's king couldn't protect them from the punishment of the king whose kingdom they violated, so that person was all alone. The punishment was determined by the violation. Some violations would bring more punishment than others. Some violations carried the death penalty and the violation that Count Dracula did was a death penalty violation.

Most people would have been killed by the king directly, but Count Dracula was killed by the king indirectly through the death of his family, which influenced him to commit suicide.

Made in the USA
San Bernardino, CA
16 February 2020